Praise for *Project M*
Step by Step

C000174760

'This straightforward and insightful approach gives results. It provides enough structure to ensure visibility and reliable delivery without smothering you with paperwork. It's no nonsense, real change for the real world.'

Matthew Dearden, President, Clear Channel Europe

'A great approach; simple to understand, yet powerful in application. It delivers the project results!'

**Dave Keighley, Managing Director,
Operations and Logistics, Virgin Media**

'An excellent introduction to project management – concise, clear and very useful.'

Mike Kelly, Partner, This Partners

'Still the best beginner's guide to project management. I know many experienced project managers who would benefit from it!'

Pat Graham, CEO, Trivaeo

'This practical guide will help you master the essentials of project management and apply them in almost any context. A refreshingly uncomplicated approach that takes you from start to finish, and delivers impressive results.'

**Victoria Pearson, Senior Director, Strategic Planning
and Corporate Communications, CNIB**

'A very simple, pragmatic and structured approach to project management. A must-have book for all new and experienced project managers.'

Anubhava Agarwal, Programme Manager, Electrolounge Limited

Project Management
Step by Step

PEARSON

At Pearson, we believe in learning – all kinds of learning for all kinds of people. Whether it's at home, in the classroom or in the workplace, learning is the key to improving our life chances.

That's why we're working with leading authors to bring you the latest thinking and best practices, so you can get better at the things that are important to you. You can learn on the page or on the move, and with content that's always crafted to help you understand quickly and apply what you've learned.

If you want to upgrade your personal skills or accelerate your career, become a more effective leader or more powerful communicator, discover new opportunities or simply find more inspiration, we can help you make progress in your work and life.

Every day our work helps learning flourish, and wherever learning flourishes, so do people.

To learn more, please visit us at **www.pearson.com/uk**

Project Management
Step by Step

How to plan and manage a highly successful project

Second edition

Richard Newton

Harlow, England • London • New York • Boston • San Francisco • Toronto • Sydney
Auckland • Singapore • Hong Kong • Tokyo • Seoul • Taipei • New Delhi
Cape Town • São Paulo • Mexico City • Madrid • Amsterdam • Munich • Paris • Milan

PEARSON EDUCATION LIMITED

Edinburgh Gate
Harlow CM20 2JE
United Kingdom
Tel: +44 (0)1279 623623
Web: www.pearson.com/uk

First published 2006 (print)
Second edition published 2016 (print and electronic)

ISBN: 978-1-292-14219-7 (print)
          978-1-292-14220-3 (PDF)
          978-1-292-14221-0 (ePub)

British Library Cataloguing-in-Publication Data
A catalogue record for the print edition is available from the British Library

Library of Congress Cataloging-in-Publication Data
Names: Newton, Richard, 1964-
Title: Project management step by step : how to plan and manage a highly
  successful project / Richard Newton.
Description: Second edition. | New York : Pearson Education, 2017. | Revised
  edition of the author's Project management step by step, 2006.
Identifiers: LCCN 2016021152 | ISBN 9781292142197 (pbk.)
Subjects: LCSH: Project management.
Classification: LCC HD69.P75 N495 2016 | DDC 658.4/04–dc23
LC record available at https://lccn.loc.gov/2016021152

10 9 8 7 6 5 4 3 2 1
20 19 18 17 16

Cover design by Two Associates

Print edition typeset in 11/14pt Times LT Pro by iEnergizer Aptara®, Ltd
Printed by Ashford Colour Press Ltd, Gosport.

NOTE THAT ANY PAGE CROSS REFERENCES REFER TO THE PRINT EDITION

This book is dedicated to Ronald H. Newton 1926–2011

Contents

3 Step 3: Create your Project Plan 46

4 Step 4: Manage delivery 101

Acknowledgements

I would like to thank all the people who have taken the time to review and feedback to me on the first edition of this book, and on any of the other books I have written. Your comments, thoughts and ideas are always appreciated.

About the author

Richard Newton is a consultant, author and speaker. He has been working on project teams, as a project manager or sponsor for almost 30 years. He has written 16 books and is a regular speaker at seminars. The common theme across all his work is a deep interest in how individuals, teams and organisations get things done. He is an advocate and practitioner of simple but robust approaches to delivering projects.

Richard currently runs two businesses: his consultancy Enixus, which provides support and coaching for organisations undertaking large projects and transformations, and Enixus Development, which supports capability development and provides business games in the areas of projects and change management – including one based on the process described in this book.

Preface to the second edition

The first edition of this book was published in 2006, having been written in 2005. As I finish this second edition it is 2016. The first edition of the book continued to be popular across a decade, yet it was getting a little long in the tooth. Nowadays, a decade is a long life for a single edition of a professional book. I was lucky to have chosen to write a book that described the fundamentals of project management, which remain relatively timeless. The types of projects may have changed, but the best ways to get things done endures.

So why the update? After 10 years, the concepts and language of business, organisations and society have moved on. Reading a book written 10 years ago makes you realise quite how much! A few examples felt dated. More specifically, the progression in thinking has been significant in project management – as typified by the emergence of Agile.

At its heart this book remains the same. It presents a simple, robust and proven approach to delivering projects, albeit refreshed and brought up to date. Apart from updating terminology there are minor changes throughout the book. Most of the examples and case studies have been revised.

I have written this version for the same four audiences who liked the first edition so much. First, it is for project managers looking for a useful, well tested way of delivering small- to medium-scale projects. Second, it is for other professionals looking for a straightforward process to control something more complex than they have led before, but without the resources to hire a professional project manager. Third, it is for organisations and project management offices (PMOs) looking for a language and a common approach that can be applied to a wide range of projects.

I have had a lot of feedback from a fourth audience. This audience is typified by students who are trying to get their head around project management before diving into the deeper end of more advanced project management tools and techniques. It also includes those who want to move into a professional project management career and use this book as a way of dipping their toes into the water.

If you are in this fourth audience I have added some specific contents for you. I have included a short extra section at the end of each chapter called 'Taking it further', which includes some thoughts on what else you could learn along with some references. I have also significantly enhanced and extended the glossary to include many common project management terms which are useful to know. This isn't because the book is not complete. It is, and you can manage a project using this approach and nothing else. But I accept you may want or need to go further and I want to help you to do this.

As always, I am happy to engage with readers of my books if there are points you want to discuss. Perhaps your feedback may help me shape a third edition some time in 2026 or beyond.

Introduction

We start with two bits of good news:

- In most situations, project management is straightforward and you can do it!

- By applying the techniques you learn in this book, you will significantly improve your chances of successfully delivering projects.

What you will be able to do once you have read the book

If you read this book, learn and practise the approach described within it, and apply it with some common sense, you will be able to:

- Manage and deliver more complex projects than you can currently without exhausting yourself or becoming overly stressed.

- Apply the principles to your personal life and find yourself completing everyday tasks more reliably.

- Come across to others you work with as competent and professional in completing your project (no headless chickens here!).

- Talk to, manage and get the best from other project managers.

How this is done

Project management, like most specialist disciplines, grows in complexity all the time. It has its own jargon, approaches, professional qualifications and societies. But you do not need all of this for most tasks. The specialist approaches are just that, specialist approaches that are powerful and useful in special situations. Most times you do not need them.

This book explains the essentials of project management in a simple way – but do not confuse simple with dumb or basic. Think of it more as straightforward and practical. This book leaves out the esoteric and highly specialised parts of project management, not because they are too complex, but because in 90 per cent of situations, you don't need them.

If you are about to start building a new high-speed railway line, sending a satellite into space or developing computer software to control all the traffic flows in a country, then yes, you do need advanced project management skills. You will need more methods, tools and skills than are explained in this book. But most tasks are not like this. There are lots of tasks that have sufficient complexity for you to worry about, that you will not be able to ensure they are completed successfully without some structure and tools, but for which the structure and tools can be simple, robust, practical and easy to use – and yet still add huge value.

Sounds familiar? Matches your need? Then you have come to the right place.

Who is this book for?

This is a book for anybody who is about to start, or who has just started, on a task that is somewhat bigger and more complex than they are used to. You may know this is a project, or you may just be realising that your normal approach of scrawling a hurried list of things to do on a piece of scrap paper to act as a memory jogger is not quite enough to make sure you get this task done.

You may have been given a project by your boss or you may be an entrepreneur creating your own projects. The project may be a conventional business project, such as launching a new product, opening a new branch or improving the way something is done. However, it may be that you're embarking on something self-initiated and non-work-related such as building a new house. The list of possible projects is endless. The common thing about these tasks is that they are complex, important – and when you start, full of unknowns.

You want to complete the task successfully, and you want to do so while looking competent and professional. What you don't have is the time, inclination or money to hire or become a professional project manager. Don't worry – this book will show you that in many cases this is not necessary, because *project management is straightforward*.

If you have some common sense, can follow a series of steps and apply them in the structured way described, and have the ability to make simple judgements, then you can manage and complete a project successfully.

You can also benefit from this book if you are starting out on a career as a professional project manager. This book will teach all the essentials that, with a bit of common sense and experience, will enable you to become a successful project manager. I'm not saying that the more specialised books do not add value, often they do, but the secret to project management is in getting the basics right. If you are a project manager who wants to be able to do projects, without filling your head with obscure jargon and overly complex models, then this is the book to start with.

Perhaps you are a senior manager in a business. Project managers work for you and you send them off to do great and important things, but you are a bit fed up with getting confused by their jargon and want to cut through to the core issues. You want to manage and get the best from your project managers, but to do this you need a better understanding of what and how they do things without spending a large amount of time becoming an expert. This book will quickly make the essentials of project management clear to you.

Finally, I have learnt from feedback from the first edition that the book is popular with students studying project management. Gaining a recognised qualification in project management will require you to go much further than this book. But if you want a friendly and reliable place to start – somewhere you can safely develop your familiarity with project management concepts before moving on to more complex writing – this will get you started.

How to use this book

This book is called *Project Management: Step by Step* because it describes project management as a series of steps. Each of the steps is immediately useful and takes you through the life of a project. The book follows the sequence of steps you should follow in completing your project.

You don't need to read this book end-to-end and then apply it. Chapter 1 provides some basic information that is helpful to understand before you get started. Chapters 2 to 5 provide the step-by-step guide to project management. You can either read a chapter at a time, applying the approach described as you learn it, or read it end-to-end and then do your project.

I have tried to avoid using project management jargon as far as possible. In many cases this is easy because the jargon is unnecessary – but in some cases I have used it. I use it because in some situations the terms are actually useful; in others because it will help in making you appear as a competent and professional project manager. Where I do this, I introduce and explain the terms in advance. In addition there is a useful Glossary at the end of the book which provides a summary of all the project management jargon used – and more!

Every chapter covers one step of the project management lifecycle, and is structured in the same way, with the following eight sections:

1. **This chapter covers.** Gives a summary of the contents of the chapter.

2. **The central point is.** Stresses the key idea(s) in the chapter.

3. **Setting the scene.** Provides some context to the content of the chapter through an example.

4. **Introduction to the topic of the chapter.** Provides all the information you need to understand the activities you will perform in this chapter.

5. **The step-by-step guide.** The core steps you must follow to complete this stage of your project.

6. **Key tips.** Key tips to remember from the chapter.

7. **To do now.** The immediate first actions to undertake to make the steps in this chapter a reality.

8. **Taking it further:** This is an optional section for those who want to learn more about project management. Project management is a rich and complex discipline. The steps in this book will enable you to deliver your project, but if you want to explore even further this section will give you a few pointers.

Each chapter is filled with examples, so the process explained is completely practical. It can be applied to any project, from a very simple, one-man activity through to a project for a team of people. The examples used vary to reflect the varying nature of different projects. Generally the examples have been selected for simplicity, but in some parts of the book clear and more complex examples are used to ensure all the details of the step-by-step guide can be shown.

Your learning process as you read each chapter will be:

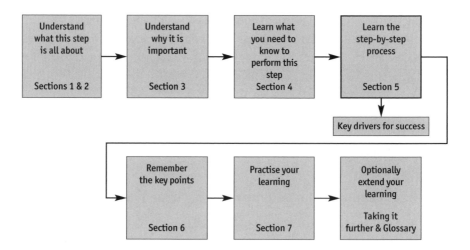

This book contains more than the steps to complete a project, as dotted throughout it are text boxes titled 'Key drivers for success'. The information in these boxes is there to support your development as a project manager. The 'Key drivers for success' focus less on the process of managing a project, but look at styles of working that will help to ensure your project is a triumph. Most people can follow a set of steps but not everyone will get the same result. If you follow the steps in this book, your project can be a success, but you can maximise your achievement by adopting certain styles of working and interacting with people as defined in the 'Key drivers for success'.

So sit back, relax and let's start your project!

Step 1

Understand the basics

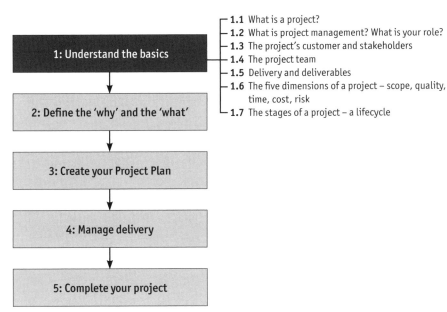

1: Understand the basics

2: Define the 'why' and the 'what'

3: Create your Project Plan

4: Manage delivery

5: Complete your project

THIS CHAPTER COVERS:

- A short explanation of some essential concepts used in project management.

> ## THE CENTRAL POINT IS:
>
> - Project management is full of jargon and concepts, many of which are unnecessary unless you are embarking on a large or complex project. However, there is some terminology and some simple project management concepts which are helpful to understand and which will aid you in fulfilling your project.

Setting the scene

When you seek assistance from an expert in any field – whether it is a garage mechanic fixing your car, a doctor advising on your health, or a company lawyer explaining some point of law – you will often find yourself listening to a set of unfamiliar words or, worse, familiar words used in unfamiliar ways. Welcome to the world of professional jargon!

Project management, like other professions, has built up its own glossary of jargon. This jargon can be helpful in some situations, but for those entering project management for the first time it can be an unnecessary barrier to understanding. This book is designed to be the step-by-step guide to project management that you can directly apply without having to become an expert project manager first. This includes minimising jargon. Where it is useful to know specific terms, I try to introduce them in the text at the most relevant points.

However, there is some jargon it is helpful to understand before going further in this book. Understanding this jargon will avoid any confusion. (Also, as a side benefit, you will be able to sound more like a professional project manager – should you wish to.) Take the few minutes to read this chapter as it will make your life a lot easier. In addition to explaining the terms, I indicate areas where professional project managers go further than the lessons in this book.

Introduction to project management jargon

There are seven pieces of jargon which are useful to understand, none of which is complex, but by understanding them you will have completed your first step in becoming a project manager.

The step-by-step guide
STEP 1 – Understanding the basics

Step 1.1 What is a project?

A project is really a very simple concept. Essentially, a project is a task with a desired end point. For example, building a new house is a project, the end point being when the house is built. Similarly, creating a new piece of software or an app is a project, as is launching a new product for a business. Projects can be used to complete many different types of tasks.

Usually the term 'project' is applied to tasks with some degree of complexity. You could argue that cooking yourself some toast is a project, with the end point being buttered toast on your plate. The word 'project' is not applied to such simple activities which do not benefit from the rigour of managing as a project. Projects have a degree of complexity. They are complex enough that just thinking through and remembering the tasks required or writing them down as a 'to do' list is not a reliable enough way to ensuring you complete them.

Projects fulfil some clear predefined objective, in a planned period of time and to a planned cost. Once the project is complete something will have changed – for example, you have a new house, a new app or a new product.

Step 1.2 What is project management? What is your role?

Project management is a formal discipline for managing projects. Project management has been developed over the past century or so as it has become apparent that without a structured approach, people are not very good at completing projects successfully. The aim of project management is to ensure that projects are completed and that the end point (the new house, computer system or new product) is achieved. More than this, project management is about reaching that end point predictably, which usually means to a given cost and within a planned amount of time.

As you read this book you will learn that successful project management is all about structure, control, sufficient attention to detail and continuously driving action. There are different approaches, or methodologies, for project management. We will not cover them in this book and you will not need to know them unless you choose to go much further in project management than this book covers. I mention them as you may hear them if you talk with a professional project manager. The names of well-known project management methodologies include Prince 2, Agile and Critical Path Method. (More information is provided in 'Taking it further' at the end of this chapter.)

Your role as the project manager is to understand enough project management to apply its rigour and structure and ensure your project is successfully completed within the time and cost you require. If you follow the steps in this book, you will find this is not so hard. The things you must do as a project manager are:

1. Ensure there is a clear understanding why a project is being done, and what it will produce.

2. Plan the project – to understand how long it will take and how much it will cost.

3. Manage the project – to ensure that as the project progresses, it achieves the objectives you have defined within the time and cost specified.

4. Complete the project properly – to make sure everything produced by the project is of the quality expected and works as required.

Key drivers for success 1 — The task and outcome focus

As a project manager there are two main things you need to be concerned with. The first is what you and the project team are doing now. What *tasks* are you completing? The second is where the tasks are leading to. What *outcome* will the tasks achieve? The first is task focus, and the second is outcome focus.

If you don't focus on the tasks required in the project, they will not get done or not be done in the way the project requires. If you don't focus on the outcome, although tasks may be completed, they will not necessarily lead to the outcome you intended.

A good analogy is with driving your car. You must focus on the task in hand of driving, or else you will crash. But you must also be thinking about where you want to get to, and so need to periodically check the map or listen to the advice of your satnav. Successful drivers do both – driving safely and getting to the place they want to.

Some project managers lose sight of one or other of these viewpoints – getting so engaged in the day-to-day tasks they forget to keep checking they are leading to the needed outcome, or getting so focused on where they need to go they forget to keep checking the necessary actions are happening. If you want to manage a project well, you need to develop the habit of switching your gaze between task and outcome repeatedly. The majority of time will be spent worrying about today's tasks, but this must not crowd out regularly checking you are heading towards your desired outcome.

Step 1.3 The project's customer and stakeholders

Every project is done because someone wants it to be done. The person who wants it to be done is called, in project management terminology, the project customer. The customer may be yourself, your boss at work, someone who buys products and services from you, or anyone else you work for or with. The customer may be one person or a group of people.

On some projects the project manager does not deal directly with the customer, but someone who represents the customer. For example on many business projects there are 'business analysts' who assess and document the customer needs into documents called 'requirements specifications'. In the Agile methodology I mentioned above, there is a role called a 'product owner', whose job it is to explain what the customer wants and prioritise them in order of importance. (More on this topic can be found in the 'Taking it further' sections at the end of this and the next chapters.)

In projects it is important to understand who the customer is and to work closely with them. Project customers have some specific responsibilities in projects. They will be involved in determining why you are going to do a project and what it will produce, for giving you access to resources such as people and money, and for making various decisions through the life of the project.

Another term you may hear in relation to projects is the 'project stake-holders'. Stakeholder is a broader term than customer, and means any-one with an interest in a project. The project customer is one type of stakeholder. For larger projects which have an effect on many people there can be many stakeholders, and there is a special discipline in pro-ject management called 'stakeholder management' for dealing with them. (More information is contained in 'Taking it further' at the end of Chapter 5.)

Step 1.4 **The project team**

The project you are about to manage will have a whole range of tasks that need to be done to complete it. For a very small project you may be both the project manager and the person who actually does all the tasks planned. For larger projects a number of people will be involved at different times in the project's life. These people are col-lectively known as the project team and it is this team that you will be managing.

There is a difference between managing people in a project team and the normal task of line management. The people in the project team usually have a line manager whom they work for on a day-to-day basis. They are only working for you on the project. They may have other tasks to complete which are nothing to do with your project. When the project ends you may have nothing further to do with the team. Even so, you need to be able to manage, motivate and direct the team. This requires you to have a clear understanding of what you need them to do in respect of the specific project you are managing and how much time they should spend on the project. Critically, you also need to make sure they are spending this time working on *your* project and not just doing other tasks for their normal manager.

The starting point to make this work is to discuss this with each team member's normal manager, and agree that the team member will be available for the project and under your management control while they are working on it.

Step 1.5 Delivery and deliverables

There is a word that project managers and people involved regularly in projects use all the time: it is delivery. Delivery in the context of projects simply means getting the things done you set out to do, and bringing the project to completion. Your role as a project manager is therefore to deliver the project.

Delivery is a useful piece of jargon as it saves having to write 'completing the project to the expected time and cost with the desired outcome' again and again!

Deliverables are what is delivered by a project – so taking the examples above, the deliverables from the respective projects are a new house, a new app or a new product. In a project the deliverables wanted are defined at the start of the project, and your success as a project manager is in delivering them in the planned time and to the expected cost.

Step 1.6 The five dimensions of a project – scope, quality, time, cost, risk

I am about to explain one of the fundamental concepts of project management. It is quite straightforward, but very useful and powerful. Spend a few minutes to make sure you understand this.

Imagine a very simple project – you are going to redecorate some rooms in your house. So you sit down and do some thinking about this decorating and decide that you will decorate your front room and your dining room, that you will use three coats of paint on every wall. You do some sums and find out that the paint will cost you £200, and it will take you four days to do the work using normal paint brushes. A friend has a machine that can spray the walls, which is much quicker. Unfortunately, it does not always work and is liable to spray paint all over the place, including any uncovered nearby furniture, so you choose not to use it. The information here has defined some important things about your project:

- You have defined the *scope*. Scope is the project manager's word for what your project encompasses. In this case your scope is to paint the front room and dining room.

- You have defined the *quality*. You have decided to use three coats of paint on all the walls. How you assess quality is relative to what a project produces; the way quality is measured will vary considerably. However, most deliverables can be created in some way with different levels of quality. By changing the level of quality, you make more or less work to produce the deliverables. Quality can be a nebulous but important concept: other examples of quality could be how robust or reliable a deliverable is, or how well presented a deliverable is. A good definition of quality is how well a deliverable fits the needs of the project customer.

- You know the *time* it will take – four days.

- You know the *cost* – £200.

- You understand the level of *risk* you want to take – you are choosing the low-risk option (painting by hand). There is an alternative high-risk option of doing it with the spray painting machine. If you choose to use this machine, you may do the work more quickly, but there are risks to your furniture and it may not work.

You may be thinking at this point – so what? The 'so what' is that these five pieces of information are not independent facts but interdependent variables. Change any one of these and you may impact the others. So, for example, change your scope and add your hall to be painted as well, and you will increase the time and the cost. However, if you subsequently reduce the quality so you use only two coats of paint on the walls, or alternatively take the risky option and use your friend's spraying machine, you may still be able to do it in the original time and cost but with the increased scope. Alternatively, by spending more money and getting in a couple of professional decorators, you may be able to reduce the time and increase the quality of the end result. There are a vast number of ways you can juggle between these five dimensions of your project.

Business projects are more complex than this but the principle still holds. Once you understand these five dimensions, you can trade them off to get the optimal result you need. For example, often in projects there are conditions set, such as the project must be done for £50k or less, or it must be completed before Christmas. If you do not think you can achieve this, then by looking at changing the scope, or the quality of your deliverables, or taking a higher-risk approach, you may be able to meet these conditions.

Risk is a particularly important concept in project management, especially as projects become larger and more complex. As tasks become more complex there are usually more uncertainties, unknowns and things that can turn out differently from how it was predicted. This is not simply a result of poor prediction, it is a basic reality of life that unknowns and risks exist. A lot of a project managers' work is spent trying to identify risks and to determine if there is anything that can be done to avoid the risks. We will only engage in simple risk management in this book. If you want to go further and become a professional project manager you will have to develop a much greater understanding of risk and risk management.

Table 1.1 shows some examples of these five dimensions for three projects, plus some sample trade-off decisions.

	Project One	Project Two	Project Three
Description	Build a development of executive homes	Set up a Christmas party for staff in the company	Upgrade the technology in the Portsmouth sales office
Dimension 1 – Scope	Five four-bedroom houses, each with a double garage.	Opening drinks, dinner and dancing for the 500 staff in the company, plus some after-dinner entertainment. Transport for staff to and from the venue to be provided.	500 tablets installed with necessary office software, sales apps and enhanced security. Staff trained how to use them.
Dimension 2 – Quality	Top-quality fittings through-out to meet expectations of people who will buy them.	Needs to be equivalent to quality of a four-star hotel.	Must be top of the range, high-specification tablets.
Dimension 3 – Time to complete	6 months from start time.	Starting on 1 November the project will complete by 20 December.	Needs to be complete by 15 September.
Dimension 4 – Cost	£2 million	£55,000	Cannot be more than £175,000.
Dimension 5 – Acceptable level of risk	Low	Medium	Low
Example trade-off decisions	• Can the quality of fittings be lowered slightly to reduce cost? • If we could expand the scope to build a sixth house, how can it be done in the same time and cost?	• It is essential that the work is completed by Christmas. At present the plan shows the project finishing on 20 December, which seems a bit close. Can we spend some more money on outside events management to ensure it happens and reduce risk? • If we need to reduce other costs to pay for the events managers, what parts of the scope can we remove?	• The plan shows that this will take until 1 October. But we could install 350 by 15 September. Can we reduce scope to 350 tablets rolled out to the top sales people first and hit the date and lower the risk of failure? We will then roll out the remaining 150 tablets after 15 September. • The plan shows it will cost £190k. However, if we reduce the specification of some of the tablets we can reduce to £175k. Is this acceptable?

Table 1.1 **Examples of the dimensions of projects**

Step 1.7 The stages of a project – a lifecycle

Every project goes through various stages in its development. These stages vary depending on the type of project. For example, a project to build a new car has different stages compared to a project to develop an advertising campaign for a new type of washing detergent. However, at a generic level projects must go through common steps such as:

1. Specifying in detail what the project is for.

2. Planning the project and working out how it will be done.

3. Doing the project and creating the deliverables according to the plan.

4. Checking that the deliverables are as you originally wanted and meet the needs.

5. Closing the project down.

These five steps defined are a simple project lifecycle. The lifecycle is a skeleton framework which you can build your project around, and Chapters 2 to 5 of this book are arranged as a straightforward lifecycle.

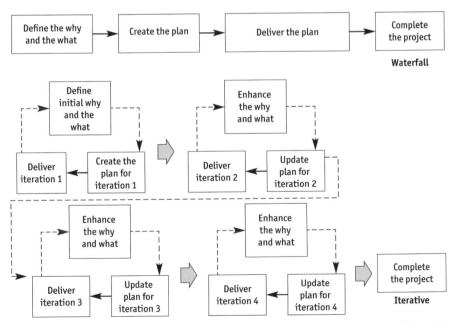

Waterfall versus Iterative lifecycle

The lifecycle of a project also depends on the methodology being used. This has been a subject of development and debate among the project management community over the last few years. For example, Agile uses a very different lifecycle from a traditional project. We will not get into this complexity in this book, but it is useful to understand the difference between a 'waterfall' and an 'iterative' lifecycle. Essentially in a waterfall project you go through the lifecycle once, doing each step once. So, applying the lifecycle shown above, you start with specifying and end with closing down the project, having done each step once in the order shown. In an iterative lifecycle, you do similar steps, but you repeatedly go through them several times. There are different reasons why you might choose a waterfall versus an iterative lifecycle. This has been the subject of hundreds of books and articles and is beyond the scope of this book to go into in any depth. But in simple terms iterative lifecycles enable you to progress quickly with prototypes with relatively simple customer requirements, and then incrementally improve the deliverables as you learn from the process of development. (More on this topic can be found in 'Taking it further' at the end of this chapter.)

You now know as much as you need to get started. You are ready to adopt the role of a project manager and begin to deliver your project. As you go through the following chapters of the book, you can literally do your project as you read.

You may find it useful to come back and read the definitions in this chapter again once you have explored some of the other material in this book.

Key tips

- Projects have a clearly defined objective which must be achieved in a set amount of time and cost. At the end, the project will have produced the predefined deliverables. The deliverables are for the project customer and are created by the project team, under the guidance of the project manager.

- Projects have five dimensions that can be flexed – the scope, the quality, the time, the cost and the level of risk taken. Be prepared to think about the optimal balance between these dimensions before you start your project.

TO DO NOW

- Check you really understand the terminology in this chapter. If possible discuss the terminology with one or two colleagues. Do you understand concepts like the 'dimensions of the project'?

- In your past experience of working on projects, what role do you normally take? Do you tend towards those tasks you associate with project management?

- If you are unsure about any of the terminology, think about the last project you were involved in (whether or not it was formally called a project):

  - What were the deliverables from the project?

  - What were the five dimensions of the project?

  - How could you have traded off between them to get a better result than you did?

  - Write down a lifecycle for any project of this type.

Taking it further: Project methods and methodologies

This is the first in a series of optional advice at the end of each step. You don't need to read this to benefit from this book fully. It is here for those who want to explore project management a little further.

This book provides a way to run projects consisting of a five-step life-cycle, some advice on completing those steps and supporting tools. Another term for this is that this book contains a project management *methodology*. I am a great believer in simple approaches that are easily understood. In the end, the success of a project is not about using the methodology, but the outcome from the project in terms of the deliverables produced and the benefits that arise from them. The methodology is a tool, not a goal in itself. However, there are situations in which richer, more complex methodologies are very helpful.

Fortunately, in project management there are many methodologies. Unfortunately, this sometimes means project managers worry more about processes and methodologies than they do about the results themselves! If you want to run complex initiatives or become a professional project manager you will need to go further than the straightforward process described in this book. Sometimes you will need to take part in debates about the most appropriate methodology. In this section I briefly introduce some richer methods you may come across.

To help, one useful concept to understand is that of a *waterfall methodology*. This is a project management methodology in which the steps are performed in a logical sequence one after another – starting at the beginning and finishing when you get to the end. As you read you will find I indicate that sometimes you may want to jump back and forth between the steps described in this book, nevertheless it is essentially a five-step waterfall method.

There are more complex waterfall methods than the one described in this book. Typically, these have more steps, and sometimes *gates* between steps. A gate is a decision point in a project at which the status is reviewed and a decision is made whether to continue the project, stop the project or do a bit more work before proceeding. For example, common early stages in business projects ending in a gate are the *concept* and the *feasibility* steps. In the concept step the idea of a project is detailed sufficiently to develop an outline business case and a concept of the outputs for the customers to review. This is done before committing to the entire project to check it is worth pursuing. Next is a feasibility step, when the ideas behind the project are further refined to give greater certainty to timescales, costs and business case. Sometimes in a feasibility step a prototype, model or simulation may be developed. Again, this enables a business to reduce risk by checking a project is really going to be successful before investing fully in it. Another common enhancement is to break what is Step 4 in this book into a series of smaller steps. This can give greater control and visibility of what is going on in a project to stakeholders.

One of the most well-known project management methodologies is Prince 2 – which stands for PRojects IN Controlled Environments, version 2. It is an entire approach which starts by ensuring that the project's goals align with business objectives through to the complete handover of deliverables. It is also a certification programme for project managers, with various levels of accreditation. It was originally pro-duced for the UK government.

There are alternatives to waterfall, most notably *iterative* methods. Iterative methods break the project up into phases. In each phase the project team may work through the entire project lifecycle, but for just some of the subset of the deliverables. Rather than producing the entire set of deliverables as one big delivery as done in waterfall, iterative methods incrementally deliver the deliverables bit-by-bit.

There are several reasons why you may choose an iterative method over a waterfall. These essentially come down to risk, change and speed to deliver benefits. One risk with the biggest of waterfall projects is that they become so complex they are unmanageable. A different risk with a big waterfall project is that it takes so long that the custom-er's needs at the end of the project are no longer what they were when it started. A third risk is that customers don't fully know what they want and that the project is subject to excessive change control slowing down and even completely stopping delivery. As for benefits delivery – a waterfall project delivers these all at the end when the full set of deliverables is complete. In an iterative project, as soon as some deliv-erables are available they can be handed over to customers to achieve some benefits.

Generally, if a project is small, the customers really know what they want and the business context is relatively stable, then waterfall meth-ods are ideal. Waterfall is also useful when the customer wants absolute commitments to time and cost for delivery, and an organisation has the capability to manage the associated risks. These criteria are not always true. Then it is worth looking at an iterative method.

One approach to projects that has become more and more important over the past few years is Agile. Agile takes the iterative approach to its extreme conclusions. Agile projects are undertaken in very short itera-tions called *sprints*. A sprint is typically two weeks long, although this timescale varies. Agile is based on the idea that changes in requirements (called 'stories' in Agile) are inevitable. The aim is to add value very quickly by delivering something of use to customers every sprint – while allowing change to happen between sprints (see section 'Taking it further' at the end of Chapter 2). Agile has proven its value in fields like software development, where it is now the predominant project methodology. It brings in a new set of language, concepts and tools from traditional waterfall project management.

Complex and particularly big projects may be defined as *programmes* (or *programs* in the United States). *Programme management* is a discipline associated with project management used to run and deliver programmes.

The term 'programme' has several definitions and is used in inconsistent ways across the project management domain. Sometimes it is just used to refer to big projects, but this is not a particularly helpful definition. A more useful definition of a programme is a family of projects that are interrelated, usually because when combined they work together to deliver a complex change in an organisation. For example, when two businesses merge there may be a post-merger programme – with separate projects looking at different aspects, such as organisational merger, IT systems merger, building and facilities merger, and so on. Each project is a self-contained project, but it usually has dependencies on other projects in the programme and only when all the projects have delivered will the programme goals be achieved.

There is a sister methodology and certification programme to Prince 2 called Managing Successful Programmes (MSP). This is a methodology for programme management.

The field of project and delivery methodologies is very vibrant with new approaches and hybrids being developed all the time. If you want to make a career as a project manager you are best served keeping yourself alert to these changes.

FURTHER READING

- **Tools and techniques for project management:** Newton, R., *Brilliant Checklists for Project Managers*, 2nd Edition, Pearson Education, 2014

- **Waterfall methods:** Mathis, B., *Prince 2 For Beginners*, CreateSpace Independent Publishing Platform, 2014

- **Agile introduction:** Rubin, K. S., *Essential Scrum: A Practical Guide to the Most Popular Agile Processes*, Addison Wesley, 2012

- **Programme management:** Snowden, R., *Managing Successful Programmes*, 4th Edition, Stationery Office, 2012

- **Overview of project management methodologies:** Newton, R., *The Practice and Theory of Project Management*, Palgrave MacMillan, 2008

Step 2

Define the 'why' and the 'what'

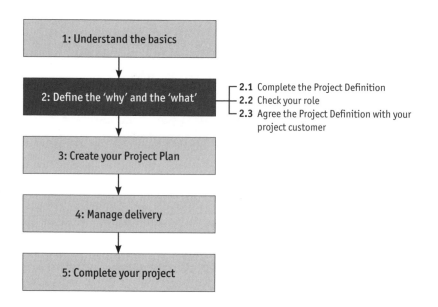

1: Understand the basics

2: Define the 'why' and the 'what'

- **2.1** Complete the Project Definition
- **2.2** Check your role
- **2.3** Agree the Project Definition with your project customer

3: Create your Project Plan

4: Manage delivery

5: Complete your project

THIS CHAPTER COVERS:

- Creating the Project Definition. This involves answering two main questions:
  - Why do you need a project?
  - What will your project deliver?

THE CENTRAL POINT IS:

- Success in projects depends on understanding precisely, completely and unambiguously what you are trying to achieve.

Setting the scene

Imagine your partner wants you to do a DIY project on your house. If they ask you to decorate part of the house, your response will probably be 'which part of the house?' The clarification is 'I want you to decorate the front room'. By asking a question, you now understand *what* you need to achieve with the project.

Underlying the request to decorate your front room is another question: *why* should you decorate it? You can complete a task only knowing what outcome you want, but it is very useful to understand also why you are to do it. The decorating might be required because you want to sell your house and the front room is looking tatty and this will reduce the selling price. Alternatively, it could be that the front room is unpleasant to sit in with its dated and scruffy decoration and, as you plan to live there for years to come, you are to redecorate it to be a really nice room to relax in. In the first case, you may decide that a quick flick round with the paint brush will be enough to convince a buyer to pay the asking price. In the latter, you may take a more critical look, do some fixing and improving before doing a top-notch decorating job.

In business, projects are usually considerably more complex than this, but the principle that there is an underlying reason why you are doing it (the 'why'), and a way you are going to achieve this (the 'what'), remains true. So, for example, if your project is to launch a new product (the 'what'), the underlying 'why' is probably something like: to increase revenues from customers in a specific segment of the market. Good project managers know that one of the core reasons they are successful is because they get clarity around why their project exists, and what it is there to do. Successful projects start by understanding clearly what the end point is.

Isn't this just common sense? Yes! But it's that sort of common sense that often gets forgotten. In this chapter I am going to explain how to understand and write the 'why' and the 'what' into a single, simple, short document called the Project Definition.

Introduction to the 'why' and 'what'

Understanding the 'why'

Everything you do you do for a reason. Doing a project should be no different. Essentially, the reason you are doing something is the answer to the question 'Why are you doing this?' 'Why?' is simple and easy to ask, yet the answer can alter what you do, how you do it, and how you think about something. It is, unfortunately, a question that we do not ask enough.

In established businesses the definition of why something is done often exists in a formal document known as a Business Case, or it may be called the Business Rationale or Business Benefit. Alternatively, it might be called the Business Objective. It may be created as an output from strategy development or a business planning exercise. Whatever it is called, you only need a concise understanding of why a project is being done – a short statement or one sentence is usually enough. The purpose is not to verify or explore the definition of why, but to get an understanding of it.

Good examples of simple, clear, concise statements of why you are doing something are:

- To increase revenues from the shops in London by 10 per cent.
- To provide the office space to expand the business in line with forecasts.
- To attract 25 per cent more customers over the summer period.
- To provide a pleasant environment to live in with enough space for a family of five.

Defining the 'why' needs to be precise. Small differences in the definition can make significant differences in what you end up doing. For example, the following two statements are quite similar, but what you would do as a result could be significantly different:

1. To improve our shops in London to increase sales per square foot.

2. To improve our shops in London to align with our high-quality brand image.

To fulfil the first, your project might fit more shelves into the shop, whereas in the second you could end up doing the opposite and having less in the shop and making it feel fashionable, airy and stylish.

A word of caution: often people start out by knowing what they are going to do, because this is what they want to do irrespective of the reason. When asked the question 'why?' they make up an answer that fits the situation and which is most palatable to the person they are talking to. This is dangerous as someone else hearing the 'why' may determine to do a completely different 'what'. For example, a business colleague may say the reason he is raising his prices is to increase his margins by 10 per cent. If he really wants to increase margins and not revenues, then this could also be done by reducing costs. If he asks someone to increase margins, on the assumption they are going to increase prices, he may be surprised when he finds that instead someone starts haggling with all the business's suppliers to reduce their prices, and hence increase margins.

The answer to the question 'why' is fundamental and should not be engineered to fit the 'what' – 'what' must be derived from it.

It is sometimes argued that if you are responsible for the 'what', you do not need to know the 'why'. Many project managers only ever discuss what the project is, and never why they are doing it. This is short-sighted. You can say you don't need to understand why you are doing something and still do it quite well. This is sometimes true, but often it is very useful to understand why you are doing something. It helps to motivate and drive you and other members of your project; most people perform better not when they blindly do things, but when they know why they are doing them. More importantly, knowing why you are doing something helps in checking that what you are doing is worthwhile and in ensuring that you make the right decisions as you go along, consistent with the 'why'.

I have seen many projects in which people have become so focused on doing *what* they planned to do, that they did the wrong things because they didn't know or lost sight of *why* they were doing it. For example, I remember a project involving moving staff from an office to a new location. Responsibility for finding and negotiating a contract on offices was duly handed out. The department responsible for new offices focused excitedly on the core negotiations with landlords. They did what they thought was a fantastic deal, and got bargain-priced offices in the new location. However, one of the reasons the project was started was to improve staff morale and retention. Staff morale and retention problems arose because of the old office location, and also because of the environment in the offices. The new offices weren't bad, but they did not live up to the expectations of an exciting new environment which had been set with the staff. By taking on cheap offices, staff morale declined rather than improved! The negotiator did a very good job if the 'why' had been what he assumed it was, 'save as much money as you can on our rent'. Had the negotiator kept his eye on the real 'why', the deal done would have been very different.

Understanding the 'what'

Once you know why you are doing your project, you need to understand what the outcome or deliverable from your project must be to enable you to achieve your 'why'. For example, if the reason why you are doing your project is to increase your company's sales, then what you must deliver is something to increase sales, such as a new product. Alternatively, if the reason why you are doing your project is to allow your business to expand, then what you must deliver is whatever will allow your business to expand, such as new larger offices.

It is obvious that to complete a project you need to understand what it is meant to deliver. However, we don't always think the obvious and too often jump into doing things without worrying if they are the right things. If you have ever started a project without understanding what the purpose is, don't worry, you are in good company. If I was given £100 for every project I have reviewed and found out that no one understood what the outcome of the project was meant to be, I would be a wealthier man!

If you get the Project Definition right, you will make the rest of your job much, much easier. If you don't, you are risking disaster. The time to get it right is now.

The step-by-step guide
STEP 2 – Defining 'why' and 'what'

Step 2.1 Complete the Project Definition

How do you go about defining what the outcome of your project is to be? This is what project managers call scope. The way you understand the 'why' and 'what' is by asking a series of simple structured questions and then by making sure that the answers are agreed with the relevant people.

The questions

The key questions you should ask are:

- *Why do you want to do this project?*

  This needs to be a clear statement of the reason why you are doing the project – what you will be able to achieve when you have done the project that you cannot achieve now.

- *What will you have at the end of this project that you don't have now?*

  This is the fundamental question. You are doing a project to deliver something. This may be some tangible object like a new house, or a new product launched; it may be something less tangible, such as creating useful new software. Finally, it may be something completely intangible such as a change in people's attitudes. (If this sounds too nebulous, consider that this is what a marketing campaign sets out to do. A marketing campaign is a project.)

  One way to think about your deliverables is to ask yourself 'How will I know when the project is finished – what will I have that I don't have now?'

- *Will you (should you) deliver anything else?*

  You know from the first question what you are setting out to deliver. However, is that really everything? If you think about it, there may be other things you need at the same time, or which it is sensible to do while you are doing the work on the main project. These need to be included in your Project Definition.

Be cautious answering this question, as the temptation can be to throw everything in and keep expanding your project. It is perfectly legitimate for the answer to this question to be 'No'. A project should not be a dumping ground for everything you might want to do. It is a structured way to achieve a specific goal. If it really makes logical sense to include other things, or if they are fundamental to achieving your original 'why', then go ahead. Otherwise say no – if your customer wants more and more put in, the response should be 'I can do anything you want, but the more you put in the more it will cost, the longer it will take, and the greater risk that something will go wrong.' That usually helps to get some focus!

- *Is anything explicitly excluded from the project?*

  Sometimes there are activities and deliverables, which for one reason or another, you want to exclude from the scope of the project, which otherwise might be thought to be included in it. It is worth being very explicit and noting these down as the scope is as much to gain an understanding of what will *not* be delivered as what will be.

You now understand both why you are doing the project and what the outcome needs to be. In Chapter 3 you will use this information to plan your project, and to work out how you will do your project. There are some important subsidiary questions to ask:

- *Are there any gaps or overlaps with other projects – or changes to the boundaries of your project?*

  Often when you start a project, you find that there is someone else doing something similar or related already. Your goal is to get something done, not to do it twice. Find out if this other project will do part of your work for you. If it will, and it will do it in the timeframe you need, you don't need to do it as well. Project managers call this a dependency on another project – we will discuss this in later chapters.

Alternatively, sometimes more than one project is kicked off at once, with the intention of the deliverables from all the projects coming together to some greater goal at the end. This set of related projects is what project managers call a programme (sometimes spelt 'program'). For example, while you are developing and launching a new product, a colleague may be re-fitting your shops to be ready to sell the new product, and another colleague may be developing sales training to help sell it. The aim is that your three projects come together so your new product goes into the shops fitted out by your colleague. Unfortunately, often when several projects like this finish and you try to make the deliverables from all the projects work together, they don't work or there is some gap.

If there are several related projects, then someone called the programme manager – essentially a super project manager – has to look at the Project Definitions for all of them and make sure the bits add up to the overall objective you have. If not, other deliverables must be added to one or more of the projects.

● *What assumptions (if any) are you making?*

We all make assumptions, if we didn't, we would never get anything done because we would be frantically proving everything before we could move on. However, when you make assumptions in a project, you should do so consciously and note them down. The problem with assumptions is that *they can be wrong*. Take an everyday life situation: when you tell your father you will visit him next Saturday you are making a series of assumptions. For example, you are assuming that nothing comes up that will stop you going and that your car will be working on Saturday. Normally you would not think too much about these sorts of assumptions. If, however, you were not visiting your father, but a key customer, and if you do not make it you may lose a £100 million contract, you will start to think through, verify these assumptions, and may even put some plan in place in case they turn out not to be true.

The same should happen in projects. I am not asking you to list literally every assumption you are making, but the important ones that may be wrong and that, if they are wrong, may alter your project.

Partially you are doing this to see if they are reasonable, but also because later on you will actively manage these assumptions as part of your project. We look at using these assumptions in Chapter 4.

Note the assumptions and ask yourself – is it really a reasonable thing to assume? Even if it is, you need to keep it visible as the state may change which can undermine your project (we will deal with this more in Chapter 4). Typical examples of assumptions that people make are:

- The operations department will provide the necessary resources to implement the deliverables at the appropriate time.

- Our existing supplier will provide the additional components necessary at or below existing prices.

- Customer behaviour in London will follow the pattern observed when we offered this service in Birmingham.

Each of these is probably reasonable, but could in some situations be wrong, and if they are wrong, they would alter the cost, timing or approach of the project.

- *Are there any significant problems you are aware of that you must overcome?*

Almost every project has some problems and challenges to overcome – if it didn't you might not need a project in the first place! When you start out you should note down anything significant. This is not an attempt to get a complete list of all possible problems but you should capture the ones you are aware of, as they may impact the way you do your project.

What does 'significant' mean in this situation? A significant problem is one that will materially affect the cost or time of the project, or change the way you approach it – and which you think there is some chance will occur.

- *Has the customer, or the situation, set any specific conditions or constraints on the way you do this project?*

If you are starting a project, it is nice to have complete freedom as to how you do it. This is rarely true. Often your customer will have a fixed time in which it must be completed, or a maximum cost. Conditions come in many forms, for example there are rules, guidelines, regulations and legislation about the way you must do some things (such as health and safety rules and industry regulations).

It is important to note you are not yet saying you can complete the project with these constraints – merely that you understand them. It is only when you plan your work out in Chapter 3 that you will actually know if it is possible.

A good way to collect the answers to the questions so far is in a simple template. Once completed, this constitutes the Project Definition. An example is shown in Table 2.1 overleaf.

The aim for the information is to be specific, precise, complete, unambiguous and concise. It should contain all the information you reasonably need to know to make a judgement about how big and complex your project is and to start planning the work. Is that every single detail? No, the real detailed requirements come later. So, taking the earlier simple decorating example, you don't need to know what colour you will paint the room. This is a detail as it does not impact making an initial judgement of how to go about painting the room, how long it will take, or how much it will cost. On the other hand, your plan will need a task to select the paint, as sometimes this can take quite some time!

Having defined what your project is about, check again. If you achieve what you have defined, will that really fulfil the reason why you are doing the project? So, for example, if your 'why' is to 'increase revenues by 10 per cent', will the things you have specified in your Project Definition really increase revenues by 10 per cent? If not, you need to go back and enhance the definition until it does.

PROJECT DEFINITION	Project name

WHY do you want to do this project?

WHAT will you have at the end that you don't have now?

Will you (should you) deliver anything else?

Is anything explicitly excluded from the project?

Are there any gaps or overlaps with other projects – or changes to the boundaries of your project?

What assumptions (if any) are you making?	
Are there any significant problems you are aware of that you must overcome?	
Has your customer, or the situation, set any conditions on the way you do this project?	

Completed on	Completed by	Agreed by

Table 2.1 The Project Definition

Here are four examples of completed Project Definitions: first for a simple decorating project, second for the more complex launch of a new product, third for an office re-fit prior to a move of staff to a new location, and fourth for a business start-up project.

PROJECT NAME/REFERENCE	Maximise house price
WHY do you want to do this project?	
– Because we want to sell our house at a maximum price and the current state of the decoration in the front room will reduce the price we get.	
WHAT will you have at the end that you don't have now?	
– We will have a newly decorated front room.	
Will you (should you) deliver anything else?	
– Yes, I will also replace the broken light fitting by the side window.	
Is anything explicitly excluded from the project?	
– I will not decorate the skirting boards or the door.	

Are there any gaps or overlaps with other projects – or changes to the boundaries of your project?	
– I will paint the left-hand wall of the hall outside the front room as this was missed out in the previous decorating project.	
What assumptions (if any) are you making?	
– The wallpaper is suitable to paint over. The paint will cover it neatly and cleanly hiding the pattern on the wallpaper.	
Are there any significant problems you are aware of that you must overcome?	
– The crack in the wall by the door needs to be plastered before it can be painted. As the plaster must be dry before decorating, this must happen at least a week before decorating starts.	
Has your customer, or the situation, set any conditions on the way you do this project?	
– I cannot work over the next weekend when we have guests. – The whole thing must be finished by September.	

Completed on	Completed by	Agreed by
26/05/16	Richard	Barbara

Table 2.2 Example of a Project Definition for a simple personal project

PROJECT NAME/REFERENCE	New product launch

WHY do you want to do this project?

– To achieve a 25 per cent increase in revenues from the consumer market, and to expand our presence in that market.

WHAT will you have at the end that you don't have now?

– We will have a new product available, consistent with our existing range, to sell into this market, with sufficient volume in store to meet the Christmas rush.

– Our shops and salesforce will be ready and trained to sell it.

– We will have the capability to handle follow-on customer support and customer service issues.

Will you (should you) deliver anything else?

– Yes, as this is the first new product we have delivered, we will document the steps I go through to speed up delivery of future products.

Is anything explicitly excluded from the project?

– We will not produce any advertising material for the product as we want it to sell by word of mouth.

Are there any gaps or overlaps with other projects – or changes to the boundaries of your project?

– We are revamping the shops in London and they will have a marketing campaign following this which there is some synergy with. We need to ensure that the new shelving they are fitting is suitable for this product.

– Additionally, when we revamp the shops, all sales staff will have refresher training. This should be used also to educate them about the new product.

What assumptions (if any) are you making?

– The market research we performed six months ago still provides a reliable view of the opportunities in the market.

– The product will expand our total share of consumer spend and will not cannibalise sales of our existing products.

– We will get a better price per unit for manufacturing costs than for existing products because of increased volumes.

Are there any significant problems you are aware of that you must overcome?

– The technology we are going to use to make the product has never been used for a consumer product. Currently it is expensive. We are certain it will work, but we need to be able to reduce the price per unit by at least 15 per cent to achieve a profitable price that we can sell the product at.

Has your customer, or the situation, set any conditions on the way you do this project?

– Ideally the product must be launched by 6 October to enable us to ship it to shops to take advantage of the ramp up in sales up to Christmas.

Completed on	Completed by	Agreed by
12/02/15	Richard Newton Project Manager	Dominic Thompson Marketing Director

Table 2.3 Example of a Project Definition for a business product launch project

PROJECT NAME/REFERENCE	Office re-fit project

WHY do you want to do this project?

– To provide suitable office space for the 100 staff in our current Logan Road offices, so we can vacate the Logan Road offices by 1 December and cease the lease on that building.

WHAT will you have at the end that you don't have now?

– We will have the office space fitted with new carpets, desks and chairs for the 100 staff, as well as the supporting connectivity and desktop equipment – plus any other miscellaneous furniture required (e.g. coat racks etc.).

Will you (should you) deliver anything else?

– No.

Is anything explicitly excluded from the project?

– Arranging the lease on the new building and generally dealing with the landlord.

– Painting and decorating of the office. (It has recently been painted and this is adequate.)

– We will not be responsible for moving staff to this office.

– We do not need to provide laptops, smartphones or tablets as these are individually allocated and staff members will bring them to the new office.

Are there any gaps or overlaps with other projects – or changes to the boundaries of your project?

– The office move project will follow on and will be responsible for configuring the wireless network around the office.

What assumptions (if any) are you making?	

– That we can complete the project in the available time window.

– The existing cabling in the building has sufficient capacity and functionality for our needs.

– There will be no additional staff-related costs following the move to the new offices.

– The existing cupboard space within the office is sufficient for our needs. We do not intend to install any new cupboards.

– We have the landlord's permission for the work we intend to carry out.

– While we are not providing laptops etc., we will need to provide docking stations, screens and keyboards to comply with the company H&S policy.

– Once we select a contractor to do the work, they will be able to start immediately.

Are there any significant problems you are aware of that you must overcome?	

– There are insufficient power sockets for the staff, so there will have to be some rewiring on the office floor.

Has your customer, or the situation, set any conditions on the way you do this project?	

– The project must be completed in time to move out of the existing premises by 1 December and must cost not more than £550k as if it does, the business case justifying the move will be invalid.

Completed on	Completed by	Agreed by
16/05/12	E Brown Project Manager	B Pierce Facilities Manager

Table 2.4 Example of a Project Definition for a business facilities project

PROJECT NAME/REFERENCE	Set up a coffee bar

WHY do you want to do this project?

– To set up a new coffee bar, which will provide a fun work environment and be sufficiently profitable to provide the income the business partners want.

WHAT will you have at the end that you don't have now?

– A fitted premise with kitchen facilities, a comfortable and welcoming café for clients, a good range of food and drinks, and an initial marketing campaign to attract customers.

Will you (should you) deliver anything else?

– Possibly: we will consider leasing a property with a flat above it. If it comes with a flat, dealing with the flat will be brought into the scope of the project.

Is anything explicitly excluded from the project?

– Health and safety, food hygiene, food preparation and other training.
– We think this may be the first of a chain of cafés, but in this project we are only considering the set up of the initial café.

Are there any gaps or overlaps with other projects – or changes to the boundaries of your project?

– James is currently working towards a Level 2 food hygiene qualification which we will need to run the café. This is outside the scope of this project, but we are dependent on it.

What assumptions (if any) are you making?	

– That we can find a suitable premise within our available budget.

– There are no planning restrictions on suitable premises in terms of converting into a café.

– We can recruit suitable staff to work in the café.

– We can find enough time within our already busy schedules to manage the project.

Are there any significant problems you are aware of that you must overcome?	

– There are plenty of cafés in the town already, so we need to stand out as something different or better than the existing cafés.

– Until the café is running we need to keep working in our current jobs to ensure continuity of income. It may be hard to run the project and keep working at the same time.

Has your customer, or the situation, set any conditions on the way you do this project?	

– The project must be completed to allow the café to start business by April 2017, in time for the town's season of festivals.

– We cannot spend more than the amount we have saved in our deposit account until we get a bank loan for the project.

– The café has to be within walking distance of home.

Completed on	Completed by	Agreed by
31/01/16	J Edwards Business founder	C Helens Business investor

Table 2.5 **Example of a Project Definition for a small business start-up project**

It really is worth reading through the examples to develop your sense of what is important in a project definition. Why not pick the one of most interest and see if you can improve it?

Step 2.2 Check your role – are you responsible for achieving the 'why' or making sure the 'what' happens?

To be successful in completing your project, you need to know what you are responsible for. Consider the simple example I started this chapter with – you are decorating the front room. Remember the reason for this was to get the asking price for the house you are selling. You must start by understanding whether you:

- Are only responsible for decorating the front room? (*what*) OR

- Are also responsible for ensuring the house achieves its asking price? (*why*)

Normally, as a project manager, you will be only formally responsible for achieving what you have specified, not why you are doing it. You should understand the 'why' but it is not your job to achieve it. Do check this though. Sometimes your customer may expect you to be responsible for the 'why'. In business this is usually called being responsible for the business benefits, or the benefits realisation. If you are responsible for the benefits, you should pretty quickly start asking yourself some subsidiary questions, such as:

- Is decorating the front room really the best way to achieve the asking price?

- If decorating the front room does not achieve the asking price, what do I do then?

If you are only responsible for decorating the front room without worrying about whether it achieves the asking price or not your life is a lot simpler! But if you are not responsible for achieving the asking price – who is?

Step 2.3 Agree the Project Definition with your project customer

Completing the Project Definition is straightforward if you are working for yourself. It takes some good quality thinking time and should not be done in a rush. Do not underestimate how much thought needs to go into your Project Definition.

If you are unclear about any of the parts think about it some more. Whenever you start a project with the definition being incomplete, you are at the very least adding to the risk it will go wrong. It is like starting to build a house without any drawings of what the end result will look like. Any mistakes you make now will be magnified by the time the project is complete – so get it right now!

Key drivers for success	**2**	Start with a customer viewpoint

As a project manager you are providing a service for the project customer. It is easy, in the drive to get the project started or the pressure to get it completed, to forget the customer. You can end up doing what you think is best irrespective of the customers' needs. The question you should always ask yourself is: are the decisions you are making and the actions you are driving really best from the project customer's viewpoint? If you don't know, ask!

When you are managing a project for someone else, completing the Project Definition can be harder. People are often surprisingly vague about what they want, other than they know they want something. Give them some time – and when you have completed a first version of the Project Definition, sit down with them and talk it through, trying to get them to understand the implications of their choices. For example, by asking questions like:

● Do you really want purple paint? Of course I can do it, but are you sure it will help sell your house?

● Do you definitely want to sell the product only in the London area – won't that inhibit overall sales?

- You want me to get new offices for the existing staff but that might not be enough for the future. Don't you want me to consider our expansion plans while I am doing this?

However, remember that it is your job to get the project done. If the customer knows what he or she wants, and has been given the chance to think through the implications of their choices, then as long as they are happy you should be too.

Sometimes customers really find it hard to define what they want, because they cannot envisage what the future might look like when the project is complete. They know they want something, but cannot imagine what it is. In these situations, there may be ways to help customers see what the future might be like without doing the full project. This is where models, prototypes and simulations can be helpful. This is a complex area beyond the scope of this book to explore fully. But essentially, each of these is a way of helping the customer start to see the future without investing all the time and effort in a full project. For example, you might create a model of a new building, a prototype of a new app or software, or a simulation of how a new process works. These are simple versions of the final deliverables, which can be used to ask questions of the customer such as:

- Does this look like what you want?

- What do you like and what do you dislike about this?

- Would this fulfil your needs or not?

- In what ways does what you want differ from this model, prototype or simulation?

Such approaches are particularly common in iterative project management and in software development. (There is more information in the 'Taking it further' sections at the end of Chapters 1 and 2).

Even if you manage to get customers to explain what they want fully and correctly there is another common problem. Unfortunately, people often change their minds and later say they want something different. This is dealt with in Chapter 4 under the topic of change management.

More annoyingly, the customer may say you are not doing what they originally asked for. To avoid this risk, ask them to sign off the Project

Definition once it is completed. This is not just about protecting yourself, but also about getting the right level of input from your customer. Experience shows that people put more effort into and take more seriously things they sign, and they are more likely to remember something written down than just said out loud.

When you have multiple customers for one project, it can be problematic to get agreement to the definition of the project. For example, a marketing person may say 'the new product you launch must be of the highest quality to be consistent with our brand', whereas a sales manager may say, 'to shift the volumes we want, we need something cheap'. Differing views about projects can be quite fundamental. You thought you were just going to deliver a project and suddenly you find yourself as the arbitrator in a dispute! Project managers often have to facilitate such negotiations. The best way is to get all the customers into one room at the same time. Go through the Project Definition line by line, discuss and work on it until you have full agreement – and get them all to sign it. This can take some time but it is time very well spent.

Key tips

- Start by understanding *why* you are doing something, then define *what* it is. Not the other way around.

- Good projects start with the end result in mind.

- Don't just think what your project is – write it down. Forcing yourself to write it down is a great way to ensure it makes sense.

- Success in developing a Project Definition requires that the information be specific, precise, complete, unambiguous and concise.

- Make sure you know if you are responsible for 'what' the project delivers or also for ensuring it achieves the 'why'. It is easier just to be responsible for the 'what', and this is normally all a project manager is responsible for.

- If you are running a project for someone else, ensure they understand the Project Definition and the implications of its contents, and get them to sign it.

TO DO NOW

- There is no better way to learn than by doing, so print off a copy of the Project Definition template (Table 2.1) and start to complete it for your project. As you fill it in, ask yourself:

  - How much detail should you go into?

  - For the project you are about to start, who are you going to work with to develop the Project Definition?

  - How are you going to ensure they agree and commit to it?

- The end result of the Project Definition should be a document that gives you enough information to really understand what the project is, and which gives your customer confidence that you really understand their needs.

- If you are having problems completing the Project Definition, practise by thinking about a project you are going to do for yourself – perhaps you will do some major DIY, have a special holiday, or want to start your own business. Try developing your own Project Definition. When you have completed it, ask yourself:

  - Which parts did you find easy to complete, and which bits hard?

  - What can you learn from this about asking project customers to complete this information?

Taking it further: Requirements

This is the second optional section of the book, for those who want to learn more about project management. It covers the topic of requirements – the formal definition of what the project customer wants.

Project managers are not expected to be experts in requirements and requirements management, but requirements are an important part of all projects. Therefore you should have a reasonable understanding of them and the associated terminology, especially if you want to run projects in business or IT.

For some projects, once you know what the deliverables are, you have all the information you need to develop them. For others, you need a series of more detailed information about the deliverables that together precisely specify the deliverables. This more detailed information is called *requirements*, and the complete collection of requirements is called the *requirements catalogue* or *requirements specification*. For example, in the case of an office re-fit, the project scope might include new furniture into the office, such as desks and chairs. This may be enough information to allow the project to be planned and managed. However, there could be some very specific additional detailed information, such as the type of chairs required, the number of drawers needed for each desk and so on. These more detailed pieces of information are examples of requirements.

Some very large or complex projects have thousands and thousands of requirements; moreover, in large businesses there is a specialist discipline, *business analysis*, whose role is primarily to analyse business problems and develop the requirements list necessary to overcome them. It is beyond the scope of this book to give a detailed description of what is in itself a specialist discipline. In large projects, for example in software development, one of the first major stages of the project is often to collect requirements, which can take many weeks in its own right.

There may be some situations in which you want to collect more detailed requirements than you would include in the Project Definition, but do not need to go to the extent of employing professional business analysts. (Remember the information in the Project Definition was there so you could scope the project, not so you know every detail of every requirement.) The aim is to get an exhaustive set of requirements that goes beyond the limited scoping information in the Project Definition and which fully defines the deliverables.

The way to develop requirements is through a series of structured interviews with your customers, to gauge exactly what it is they want from the project. If you ask people what they want delivered, they may go on giving you far more requirements than you can possibly deliver. So it is important to understand that every requirement typically adds some time and some cost to the project. Therefore when people are giving you requirements, you should understand whether these are:

- *Must have.* The project will not be complete without them, and your customer will not be satisfied without them. Unless all the mandatory requirements are met by the end deliverables from the project, it is a failure.

- *Should have.* While not mandatory, these are requirements the customer really wants you to fulfil, and unless there is a good reason, usually in terms of unacceptable extra cost or time to the project, you will try to deliver these as well.

- *Could have.* Requirements the customer wants you to fulfil if it is reasonably straightforward, but will not be too worried if you cannot.

- *Would like, but won't get.* Requirements that the customer would like, but cannot be delivered by this project and will not cause problems if they are not delivered.

- There is a simple acronym to remember this: **MoSCoW** (must, should, could, would). A simple example requirements catalogue is shown in Table 2.6.

No.	Requirement description	M	S	C
1	Each member of staff will have a suitable office chair that conforms to our business standards.	✓		
2	Each member of staff will have a desk with an integrated drawer unit, space to work on and space for a laptop with an independent wireless screen and keyboard.	✓		
3	Each member of staff will have additional storage space for two archive boxes near their desk.		✓	
4	For every four members of staff there will be an additional chair for visitors.		✓	
5	There will be five additional tables which can take up to four chairs for informal meetings.	✓		
6	The six secretaries' desks will have a second drawer unit to account for the additional paperwork they deal with.			✓

Key:
M = Must have, S = Should have; C = Could have

Table 2.6 **Example of a simple requirements catalogue**

There are alternative ways to collect and deal with requirements. In the 'Taking it further' section in Step 1, I introduced the concept of iterative project management methodologies, and specifically Agile. These approaches often started with dissatisfaction with the traditional requirements analysis and collection phases of projects – and the regular risk of poor requirements resulting either in poor deliverables or excessive change in requirements.

In an Agile sprint, the team works to a set of *stories*. Stories are a specific way Agile defines requirements. At the beginning of each sprint the stories are reviewed. They are reviewed in a prioritised list produced by the *product owner*, called the *backlog*. The product owner acts as the single point interface between the team and the customers – defining and prioritising the stories. Once the stories are reviewed the team commits to delivering some set of stories within the next sprint. Product owners cannot change the stories to be delivered in the sprint once it is started, but they can add stories for the next sprint and reprioritise the backlog for future sprints. In this way Agile is flexible to change relatively quickly, while giving the team a fixed set of deliverables to produce in the short term.

FURTHER READING

- **Business analysis:** Cadle, J., Eva, M., Hindle, K., Paul, D., Turner, P., Rollason, C. and Yeates, D., *Business Analysis*, 3rd Edition, BCS, 2014

- **Stories:** Cohn, M., *User Stories Applied: For Agile Software Development*, Addison Wesley, 2004

Step 3

Create your Project Plan

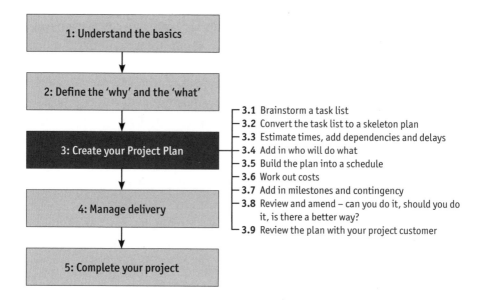

1: Understand the basics

2: Define the 'why' and the 'what'

3: Create your Project Plan

3.1 Brainstorm a task list
3.2 Convert the task list to a skeleton plan
3.3 Estimate times, add dependencies and delays
3.4 Add in who will do what
3.5 Build the plan into a schedule
3.6 Work out costs
3.7 Add in milestones and contingency
3.8 Review and amend – can you do it, should you do it, is there a better way?
3.9 Review the plan with your project customer

4: Manage delivery

5: Complete your project

THIS CHAPTER COVERS:

- Creating the Project Plan. The Project Plan shows *how* to do your project, and from it you can see how long the project will take and how much it will cost.

- Checking that your project is possible (*can you do it?*) and that it makes business sense (*should you do it?*).

Developing a Project Plan is explained through a detailed example in the section of this chapter titled 'The step-by-step guide'. The approach presented can be used for simple and complex projects. To ensure that all the different considerations in developing a Project Plan are covered, the example is slightly more complex than in the previous chapters. This is because planning is probably the most unfamiliar task to those new to project management. If you take the time to understand this chapter, you will see the approach explained is straightforward. Having grasped it, you will understand the most complex part of this book.

THE CENTRAL POINT IS:

● Project management is concerned with ensuring you achieve your objectives to a predicted time and cost. The basis for doing this is to understand clearly how you will do your project. This understanding comes by developing a Project Plan.

Setting the scene

Imagine that you are about to sign a contract with one of your suppliers to do some work for your business, perhaps developing new software or re-fitting a chain of shops. Alternatively, in your private life you may ask a builder to do some work on your house. Whichever example you consider, you are about to ask the supplier to do a project for you. Imagine you have already agreed what this project will deliver using the approach described in Chapter 2. You know you will get what you want. What more information do you want from the supplier before you commit to the contract? The most important questions you will have usually are: 'How long will this work take?' and 'How much will it cost?'

Instead of thinking about someone doing a project for you, imagine you are doing a project for someone else. They want to know how long you will take and how much you will charge. To answer these questions you need to understand how you will do the project and how much it will cost. The answers to these questions are found by developing a Project Plan.

Project Plans do not always provide the answer you want to hear. For example, you may have a condition that the project is to be completed by the end of May, but a plan shows it will take until the end of July. Alternatively, you may have a maximum of £100k to spend on your project, but a plan shows it will cost £250k. The Project Plan enables you to check that you can do the work within the conditions defined, and that it makes sense for you to do it.

Project Plans sit at the core of managing projects and so this is the longest chapter in the book. You may find it best to read this chapter a bit at a time, rather than trying to go through it all in one go. There are lots of tables in this chapter which makes it look more complex than it is. Don't be intimidated by the tables: in reality, there is one main table, which is built up in steps and so is shown several times as each step builds up.

Good planning enables a project manager to take the understanding of what is to be delivered and reliably make this happen to a predicted cost and time. Doing any complex task without planning first means you do not know how long it will take and how much it will cost – and such predictability is often essential. More critically, without a plan your ability to meet the original objectives of the project (the 'why' and the 'what') is uncertain. Without a plan you are stepping out into the dark.

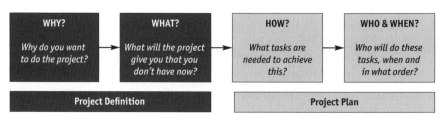

The logic of project management

Introduction to the Project Plan and estimating

The next few pages of this chapter provide an introduction to project planning and estimating. They present the information you need to understand before you create your Project Plan. The subsequent section then applies this knowledge and presents the actual steps to develop a plan through a detailed worked example.

How you will do your project and achieve your objective is defined in the Project Plan. At one level, a Project Plan is just the list of tasks you need to do to complete your project. Essentially, this plan shows the order of the tasks, the length of time each task will take, and who is responsible for doing each one. The plan is used for many things, but most importantly:

- It enables you to understand how long a project will take, and how much it will cost to do.

- It provides information you can use to explain the project to other people.

- It allows you to allocate work to different people in the project. A plan is as much a tool for work allocation and management of people, as for understanding the length of time it will take.

- It is the basis for managing your project to a successful completion (as will be described in Chapter 4).

Professional project managers have a huge set of tools and usually some helpful experience to produce plans. The work to produce the plan for a major programme of work requires skill and expertise, but the fundamental activities in producing a plan are not that complex and are easy to apply for reasonable-sized projects. Planning builds on the normal human approach of breaking problems that are too large to resolve in one go into smaller chunks. This process is called decomposition by project managers.

I am first going to define the logical activities in producing a plan, and then I shall describe how to create a plan in practice. The six activities in producing a plan are to:

1. Divide the overall project into its component tasks, and continue to divide the component tasks into smaller tasks until you have a comprehensive list of things that must be done to complete the project.

2. Estimate the length of time each task will take.

3. Order the tasks into the right sequence.

4. Determine the people, money and other resources you need to do the tasks in the plan.

5. Check what resources are available and refine your plan to take account of this. Once you have done this you have a complete plan.

6. Review the plan – does it match your needs? Looking at the plan – can you actually do it, and should you do it?

The six activities are shown here as a simple logical sequence. In practice, you will go through these activities several times before your plan is in a state you are fully happy with. Before you start to develop your plan, I introduce these topics in more detail.

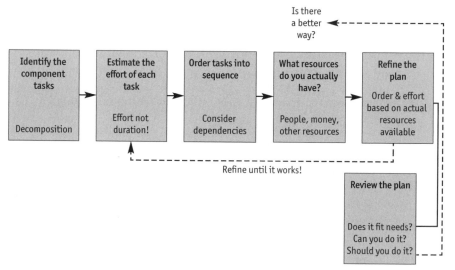

The logic of project planning

The component tasks and milestones

Breaking big activities into component tasks is something we all do all the time. Whether it is as simple as planning a trip to London – thinking about the tasks of driving to the station, taking the train to Paddington, and then using the Underground to the final destination – or a complex activity that breaks into hundreds of tasks, decomposition is something we all do naturally. However, in a project it is generally more complicated than the activities you are familiar with on a day-to-day basis.

Breaking down a major project into the relevant tasks requires clear thinking and effort. Determining the task breakdown enables you to bring experience to bear, whether it is your own or anyone else's familiar with the type of project you are planning.

People new to project planning often struggle to understand what level of detail to go into in breaking tasks down. This is a subjective judgement and there are no hard and fast rules, but remember the purpose of the plan: you are creating a structure whereby you can estimate times and costs, allocate work to people and manage delivery. You are not defining a detailed step-by-step instruction for carrying out each of the tasks in the plan. The questions to ask once you have broken your work into its component tasks are:

● Is it enough to help you manage and allocate the work?

● Does the detail help you estimate and schedule the project?

Consider three different task breakdowns for a decorating project (Table 3.1).

The information in the left-hand column is not sufficient to work out the cost and time to do the project. On the other hand, that in the right-hand column is too much. It's not that it's wrong, just that you don't need this level of detail to plan. The middle column seems about right.

Insufficient detail	Sufficient detail	Too much detail
Decorate room.	Select colour.	Go to DIY store.
	Buy sufficient paint.	Look at the colours available.
	Prepare walls.	Get sample pots of paint.
	Paint first coat.	Try on wall.
	Paint second coat.	Wait for it to dry.
	Final touch up.	Select option.
		Estimate how much paint you want.
		Return to DIY store.
		Buy paint.
		Survey walls.
		Identify all bits of walls that need to be fixed.
		Mark the places to fix.
		Fill cracks.
		Fix paper etc.

Table 3.1 **Example of task decompositions**

If your project lasts any length of time, especially if it is over a month and you are inexperienced, it is helpful to add some milestones. Milestones are points in a project that identify when you have completed an important stage of the project. Once you start to manage a project, you will find that the detailed tasks tend to shift around. The milestones should not. They are useful to track progress at a high level and to communicate to people outside of the project – to understand where you are in project progress without needing to know the details. They are not activities in their own right, but reflect the completion of a series of activities and the production of key deliverables. One milestone a month is a good rule of thumb. Examples of possible milestones for three projects are shown in Table 3.2.

	Project One	**Project Two**	**Project Three**
Project description	**Building your own house**	**Developing a smartphone app**	**Producing a short film in a school**
Possible milestones	1) Completion of foundations. 2) Completion of walls and roof. 3) Completion of internal walls, plumbing and electrics. 4) Completion of internal fitting and decorating.	1) Requirements gathered. 2) App designed. 3) Code written. 4) System tested. 5) Bugs fixed and app handed over for live use.	1) Script finalised. 2) Cast selected. 3) Script learnt. 4) Filming completed. 5) Editing completed. 6) Film shown.

Table 3.2 Examples of milestones

Estimating time

The part of planning that people usually find the hardest is estimating how long the project will take. Accurate estimating can be difficult. Most people are not naturally good at it. This is because they don't know how to do it. With a suitable approach, most people can estimate sufficiently well.

The first thing to help put your mind at rest is that while it is helpful for your estimates to be accurate, you should not worry about getting them exactly right. They are inherently uncertain, as any judgement about the future is. If you try to make perfect estimates you will spend more time estimating than doing anything else on your project. Estimation is as much an art as it is an accurate science. It is best done with experience of doing similar tasks before.

The next thing to clarify is what you are estimating. Your estimates should be the effort it takes to do a task, not a guess as to how long it will take before you have completed the task (which is the duration). This is a subtle but critical difference.

The effort is how much time you must spend working on something to complete it. The duration is how long it takes you to get around to doing it. It may, for example, take you one hour to read a business report (the effort). If you start reading it, then go off and do something else for four hours and then complete reading it, the time to complete the task will be five hours. The duration is five hours. In planning you should only be interested in the effort to do the reading – one hour. The beauty of planning is that the duration will be derived automatically when you look at the sequence of events you need to do in the project.

The next thing about estimates is that they should be a judgement of how long a task takes *normally*. What is a reasonable length of time to do it in? Most tasks take different lengths of time in different situations. For example, it may take you typically two days to read a book if you read it without interruption – but some books will take half a day, and some will take four days. If I ask you how long will it take you to read 100 books, you may think – anything between 50 and 400 days. When planning, use the average time at two days per book; this gives a total for 100 books of 200 days.

You may be thinking, but doesn't that mean I risk running out of time in the project? Yes, but this is dealt with by something called contingency, which will be explained later. In practice, when people are asked for estimates, they often give the maximum time a task takes. If you do this, your plan will stretch out for much, much longer than the project will almost always take.

The unit of time being estimated depends on the size and scale of the project. You may estimate in terms of hours, days, weeks, months or years. The units of estimation can be person-hours, person-days, person-weeks, person-months, etc. – where a person-hour is the amount of work one person can do in an hour, a person-week is the amount of work one person can do in one week, and so on. In practice, estimating to person-days is normally sufficiently accurate for a small to quite large project. Estimating to person-hours usually just gives a spurious feel of accuracy. In fact, if you are doing this, you have probably gone into too much detail in your task breakdown. For larger projects person-weeks, or just possibly person-months of effort are usually sufficient. Person-years are never accurate enough.

But what if you really don't know how long a task will take? There are many ways of estimating task durations, but essentially you have five options:

1. *Ask someone who does know.* This is the best option. Experience is usually the best way to estimate.

2. *Use any available rules of thumb.* For instance, if it takes about 1½ hours to install a new light fitting in an office, someone should be able to install about six a day. To install 100 will take about 17 days for someone allocated full-time to this task.

3. *Model it against other similar tasks.* If you don't know anyone who has done this, have you ever done anything similar? How long did that take?

4. *Break the task down further until you get tasks you can estimate.* This approach works in situations in which a more detailed breakdown gives clarity. However, if you are getting to a set of tiny tasks that each take an hour or two, you are going too far. To an extent, by breaking down tasks into smaller chunks, you make estimation easier. However, at some stage you have to make an

estimate, and guessing the length of 10 small tasks is inherently no more accurate than guessing the length of one big task!

5. *Make an assumption.* At this stage an assumption is nothing more than an educated guess as to how long it will take. If you have no better information, do this.

Having planned your tasks and estimated their lengths, you can create a first-cut plan. However, you may be concerned about errors you have made in planning. You may also be concerned that in real life things may go wrong – how do you deal with this? You deal with this by setting aside a pot of money and time that you will try not to use, but will resort to only if there are problems. This is called contingency.

The amount of contingency you set aside depends on how risky the project is and how much experience you have of doing similar things. For low-risk projects, doing things you are familiar with, a contingency of 5–10 per cent for time and money is normally enough. For higher-risk projects, you may want to leave a contingency of 20–25 per cent, and for very high risk and unfamiliar tasks it may be 50 per cent or more.

You may think – isn't this just cheating or a sign of poor planning on behalf of the project manager? No, it's not. Contingency will not be used unless it is really needed, and it is there because a good project manager knows he or she cannot predict the future with 100 per cent accuracy, especially for a high-risk or unfamiliar task.

The importance of contingency also depends on what happens once your project is finished. If it is a personal project and it does not really matter if it is a little late, or over budget, and you are using project management simply because it is a complex task and you want to be sure it gets done, then you do not need to worry about contingency. If it is a critical project that once you have completed someone else will immediately start some major business initiative, you want to be sure that the date you give as the end date is achievable. This requires giving yourself some buffer in the form of contingency. Having such a buffer is not being overcautious, it is sensible management.

Ordering the tasks

If your project breaks down into 100 tasks you can, in theory, start all 100 tasks at the same time. The project will take as long as the longest task. There are two problems with this idea:

- You can only do so many things at a time. Tasks have to wait until you are free to do them.

- There are dependencies between some tasks.

A dependency is a link between activities, which means that they can only be done in a certain order. For example, for me to drive my car it has to have an energy source – the task of driving is dependent on the task of filling up with petrol or charging the batteries. There are many forms of dependency. In practice, you mostly need to think about predecessor dependencies. What tasks have to be completed (or started) before another task can be started? These are shown on your plan as predecessors.

One specific type of predecessor you need to be aware of is an external dependency. This is a dependency on a task that is not being done within your project or under your management. For instance, consider the situation in which you are running a project to design and build some new houses, and you are not involved in buying the land to build them on or in getting planning permission for the building. All the tasks involved in selecting and buying land, and applying for and gaining planning permission are outside of your project and will not appear in your Project Plan. However, you still have a dependency on them. You cannot build without the land or the planning permission. The order of your tasks has to reflect when the necessary external predecessor tasks are complete. (The external dependencies should have been identified in your Project Definition.)

When you review your plan, you can find tasks that prompt you to think: 'Oh, I can do half of the task and then I need to wait a week while something else happens before I can complete it.' Divide such a task into two parts. A good example of this is when you have to order something from a supplier. If your project requires you to install new video conference (VC) facilities in an existing office, you will have a task to install the VC equipment which is dependent on the supply of new screens. As part of this task, you will remove the old existing screens as well. You cannot install the new screen until you have received them from your supplier, but you could remove the old screens. Split the task into two halves. The first half of the task (Remove the old screens), can be done straight away, and the second half (Install new screens) waits until the completion of the predecessor task (Supply new screens).

It is important to differentiate between tasks that have been ordered because they have predecessors and tasks that are ordered to take account of the availability of people to do the work. In the latter situation a project can sometimes be speeded up by using more people, whereas in the former it cannot.

You may think simply adding more people will always speed up your project. It often will do, but beware. Not all tasks can be broken into many pieces for different people. Remember the project management aphorism: 'It takes one woman nine months to have a baby, but nine people cannot have a baby in one month.'

The people in your project team

Once you have a task list you are in a position to identify who you need in your project team. You probably had a good idea of who will do the project work prior to completing the Project Plan. However, it's important that you get the right project team. Without the right team, no matter how good a plan you have, the work will not get done. When choosing the people to work on your project, consider six things:

1. What skills are required – and what skills do the people you are choosing have? You are looking for a match between your needs and the skills of the people chosen.

2. How many people with each type of skill do you need?

3. Which people have these skills?

4. Are they available? It is no good trying to run a project with people who are 100 per cent busy on other work.

5. Can you afford them? People usually do not work for free, and different people usually are paid different salaries. If you have to

pay for people from your project budget, can you afford the people you have chosen?

6. Do they have the right attitude? This is often forgotten, but you don't only want people with the right skills available and affordable for your work, but you want people who want to be involved in your project. A person who wants to be involved and is energetic and excited by the work will often produce more than a higher skilled individual who is not interested.

As the project manager, you are a member of the project team. Do not underestimate the work of managing the project. On a small project you can be a part-time project manager and also be allocated some of the tasks in the plan. On a large project, the job of managing the work will take 100 per cent of your time. You will not have the time to be doing any of the individual tasks as well.

Dealing with costs

The costs of a project fall into two main categories:

- *Costs associated with doing the work on the project.* This is usually mostly people's time working on the project. It may also include things you have to buy or rent to do the project. For example, you may rent a room for a couple of months for the project team to work in. You buy some project management software to help you run the project.

- *Costs associated with things you must buy to create the deliverables.* For instance, if the project is to do with building some houses, this would include cement and bricks; if your project was to develop a new computer service, it would include buying computers and software.

I am not going to deal with the accounting treatment of these costs. Usually, this is left to the accountants, and project managers need just worry about how much money they need. However, it is helpful to identify variable costs that depend on how much of something you use or buy, and fixed costs which you have to pay irrespective of how much you use. To calculate the cost, identify all the variable and fixed cost elements.

The budget you need for a project is the total of the costs of all of these elements. Some organisations do not allocate the cost of staff time to the project. In the detailed example I provide below, I have charged people's time. This is good practice as it encourages you to make sure that people do things in the time you expect of them. If you are charging staff time to your project, don't forget to include your own time as project manager.

Usually some costs are known or can be easily looked up, such as the cost of booking a hotel room. Other costs need to be estimated, and most of the same principles used for estimating time hold. Where possible ask someone with experience. Where this is not possible, you must make an assumption and estimate the cost to the best of your ability. The more you need to guess costs, the more risk that the budget will be wrong, and the more contingency you should have.

Can you do the project; should you do the project?

Once you have a Project Plan and a view of the time and cost of a project, you may feel it is time to get started. Almost, but you need to ask yourself a couple of important questions:

1. *Can you do the project?* Is it possible? If your plan shows you need 50 people to do your project and you only have 10, or it will cost £1 million and you only have £100,000, then it is not possible – or at least not possible in the way you are proposing.

2. *Should you do the project?* Is it viable and economically sensible? Do you meet the conditions you set yourself? Is there a maximum time or cost you need it done within? If you do the project, will you meet your original 'why'? Imagine your project was being done to reduce costs by £400k, and your plan shows the project will cost £2 million to do. If you have £2 million, then you have the money to do it, so you can. However, you probably should *not* do it as the cost saving (£400k) is a lot less than it will cost to achieve (£2 million).

Sometimes all planning does is make you understand that something you want to do is not possible. If your plan shows this, don't despair. You should think whether anything can be changed to meet your conditions. For instance, if the condition you cannot meet is that the project must be completed in a limited amount of time, can you do it faster by spending more money? If it is to do the project for a limited amount of money, can you do it more cheaply – by reducing the scope, lowering the quality, or taking more risk?

Although project management will significantly improve your chances of doing a complicated task well, it won't make the impossible possible. It is far better that you know the truth now rather than spending time and money on a project only to find out that you cannot do it. In business the concept of 'failing fast' is often discussed. This is the view that if you are going to fail at something, you should do it quickly, learn from it and then try something else. Planning helps you to fail fast!

Even if your project can be done and should be done, you must review your plan and check to see if it is the best way to achieve your objective. A first pass plan is rarely the best way of doing something.

Developing a Project Plan in practice

In the next section I explain the actual steps to develop a Project Plan. The first time you develop a plan you may find it complicated. You may ask yourself all the time, is this good enough? The amount of time and effort you spend planning is a judgement and depends on the complexity of a project. Some project managers do it quickly, while others spend up to 30 per cent of the total project time getting the plan right. It is a trade-off between lengthy planning for perfect accuracy versus going too quickly and producing something meaningless. Planning is a valuable activity. The better your plan, the easier and more reliable your project will be. But remember that the Project Plan is a tool to help you deliver the project and not an end in itself.

There are many software packages, for instance MS-Project, that can help you in implementing the approach described in this chapter. I have assumed you do not have any such tool and will work using some simple forms. If you do have project management software, it is a good idea to use the forms once as it will help you to understand project planning more fully. Great as the software tools are, and successful as they are in helping people to manage the planning process, they will not ensure you create a good plan. That requires your clear and structured thinking.

The step-by-step guide
STEP 3 – Creating your Project Plan

In the previous section you learnt all you need to know to be able to create a Project Plan. This section turns this information into a practical and straightforward process for planning. It is explained via a worked example. The example is a little more complex than in previous chapters to ensure it shows all the different nuances of planning. Work through it with a little care and you will have completed the most complex part of this book.

There are many varieties of projects. Every reader of this book may use it to run a different type of project. The example used has been chosen because it requires no special expertise to understand. Many project plans will have tasks in them that unless you are an expert in that field you will not understand fully. The aim of this example is not to make you an expert in the type of project discussed, but to understand the underlying process required to plan a project.

Step 3.1 Brainstorm a task list

Start to develop your Project Plan by brainstorming a list of the tasks you need to do to complete the project. Your aim is to get close to a complete set of tasks roughly in the order in which they need to be done. You can do this by yourself, but it is better to involve others whom you think could help. In practice, I don't advise running a brainstorm with more than six people. Unless you are good at facilitating brainstorms, it will turn into more of a debate than a brainstorm. If you know anyone who has done a similar project before, try to involve them as their experience will be valuable.

Key drivers for success	**3**	Develop an end-to-end perspective

It is obvious that successful projects are not those that complete some of the tasks, but are those that complete *all* of the necessary tasks. Yet, project managers do not always think from an end-to-end perspective. By this I mean one in which they are continuously thinking: What is left to be done? Is that all the things that need to be done? Is there still enough time in the plan, and money in

▶

the budget to do everything required to ensure success? Is there anything that may have been forgotten? An end-to-end perspective is about thinking holistically about the whole project and not just the things you are doing at this precise point in time.

Having an end-to-end perspective is about looking back over the work you have completed and checking it is sufficient to move the project towards the end goal and that nothing has been left out. Even more important, an end-to-end perspective is about regularly looking forward and ensuring that the plan is complete and the budget is enough. From the first day you start your project and build the plan, you should ensure you are thinking about all the things to reach your end goal. Tasks of the type described in Chapter 5 do not get forgotten in the plans of project managers who take an end-to-end perspective.

It is unlikely that you will produce a complete set of tasks at first, nor will you put them all in the correct order. Ideally, you should do this in a way that enables you to add more tasks as you think of them and rearrange the order several times. (That's when planning software is really helpful.)

A good and simple way to do this is to write each task on a Post-it note. Each Post-it should have only one task on it. As you create them, stick these onto a wall. At first this may be difficult, but once you have stuck a few tasks up, you will find your mind starts to generate more and more tasks.

When you have created a set of tasks on the wall, group the common ones together. What you are looking for here are related tasks – or better still, the hierarchy of tasks. A hierarchy of tasks shows the decomposition of a major task into more minor tasks. For example, you may have a major task 'Set up new office for a growing business', which breaks down into a series of sub-tasks such as: 'Identify and select office'; 'Fit out new office'; and 'Arrange move from existing offices'. There may be several layers of sub-tasks. Put these groups of tasks into what seems like the most logical ordering.

Once you have your Post-it notes ordered on the wall, this is your first pass of a rough-cut plan. The picture of the project will be clearer, but will remain incomplete. Ask yourself:

1. Are these really all the tasks you need to meet your objective? If not, add the missing tasks and fit them in where appropriate.

2. Are all the tasks at a sufficient level to help you understand and be able to allocate to someone and then manage the task? If not, break down the tasks into smaller pieces until you really start to see all the activities. Keep on repeating this until you feel you have all the tasks needed at a level that enables you to see what needs to be done to deliver the plan.

3. Is everything here really necessary to meet the objective or are some extra? If any tasks are additional to meeting your objective, remove them. In a brainstorming session you will often create tasks that are not really part of your project.

4. Are all the tasks different or are any really the same? If any tasks are the same, remove one of them. Alternatively, if two tasks overlap, redefine them so they are distinct separate activities. (For example, the tasks 'Train all sales staff' and 'Train all staff in London' overlap for London sales staff. Rewrite them so they are separate tasks.)

Once you have a task list you are happy with, number the tasks in the order you have them. Literally, start at 1 and increment by 1 for each additional task. Put this number in the top left-hand corner of the Post-it. This is the task number. Now you are going to number the tasks again, but this time taking account of the hierarchy of tasks. This is called the Work Breakdown Structure, or WBS number. Start by numbering the first task with a 1 again in the top right-hand corner of the Post-it. Now if this task has any sub-tasks, number them 1.1, 1.2, 1.3 and so on. If any of these has sub-sub-tasks, number them in the format 1.1.1, 1.1.2, 1.1.3 and so on.

The WBS number is what you will use in managing the project and is explained below. The task number is simply there for administration. The WBS number is essential. You don't absolutely need the task number, but I always have one. The task number helps with handling your Post-it notes, making it obvious if you have lost one – for instance if you drop the pile.

Let's start our example. Consider a project that involves improving some office space that your business has just taken over, which will be used by the 100 staff you have. The Project Definition for this project was produced in the last chapter – see Table 2.4.

You want to run this project yourself but need some specialist help, therefore you will choose a contractor to work with on the project. You are planning to do some rearranging of the office, which may require new lights and new power sockets for staff. You want everyone to have new improved furniture and better desktop equipment. Everyone already has a laptop, and you want now to provide a docking station the laptops can connect to. This docking station connects in turn to larger screens and keyboards so everyone can work comfortably. Your contractor will help with the office and the furniture, but you can sort out the desktop equipment yourself using your existing IT staff. The set of Post-it notes you have created and organised could look like the figure below.

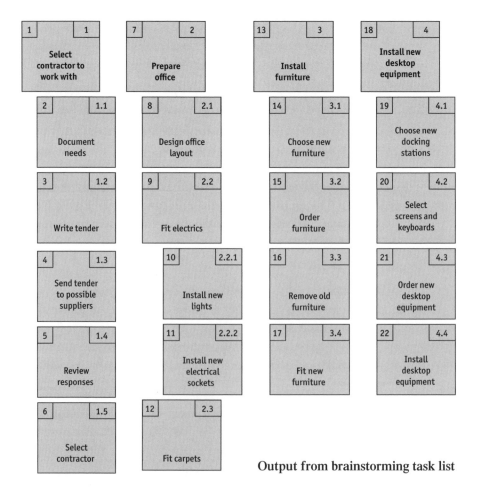

Output from brainstorming task list

At this stage, do not worry too much about who will do the work, or whether the order is absolutely correct.

Step 3.2 Convert the task list to a skeleton plan

The task breakdown you have produced on Post-it notes is now going to be transferred into your plan. When documented, this is called the Work Breakdown Structure by project managers. There is a lot more information in a plan other than this WBS, but it provides the skeleton which all the other information is built upon.

You will transfer the information from the Post-it notes on to a form. When you transfer the information, you may find you need to rename some of the tasks for greater clarity. You will also find that as you write them down, you think of more tasks to be added.

Over the next few subsections I am going to show you how to complete a plan, building the information into a table. I will build this table a few columns at a time until you have a completed plan. The first three columns simply use the information directly from the Post-it notes. By doing this you will get something that looks similar to Table 3.3.

Task number	WBS number	Task description
1.	1	Select contractor to work with
2.	1.1	Document needs (what you want the contractor to do)
3.	1.2	Write tender (convert needs to a formal tender document)
4.	1.3	Select possible contractors
5.	1.4	Send to possible contractors
6.	1.5	Review responses
7.	1.6	Select contractor
8.	2	Prepare office
9.	2.1	Design office layout
10.	2.2	Fit electrics
11.	2.2.1	Install new lights
12.	2.2.2	Install new sockets
13.	2.3	Fit carpets

▶

Task number	WBS number	Task description
14.	2.4	Install wireless network
15.	3	Install furniture
16.	3.1	Choose new furniture
17.	3.2	Order furniture
18.	3.3	Remove old furniture
19.	3.4	Fit new furniture
20.	4	Install new desktop equipment
21.	4.1	Choose new docking stations
22.	4.2	Select screens and keyboards
23.	4.3	Order new desktop equipment
24.	4.4	Install desktop equipment
25.	5	Test and handover
26.	5.1	Test working of wireless LAN
27.	5.2	Allocate desks to staff
28.	5.3	Support staff as they set up at desks

Table 3.3 **Example initial skeleton plan**

When you see the information in a format like this, it may trigger further thought about the Project Plan. Again ask yourself:

● Are these really all the tasks you need to meet your objective? (Check and review the Project Definition.)

● Is there anything you need to do at the end of the project that you have not yet included? At this stage it is worth jumping ahead and quickly checking Chapter 5. There are some tasks to perform at the end of a project which are often forgotten, but which need to be included in the plan and budget.

● Are all the tasks at a sufficient level to help you understand and be able to manage the task?

● Is everything here really necessary to meet the objective or are some tasks extra?

Then take the necessary action. At this point you should be striving for completeness. If you are observant, you will notice I have added several additional tasks into the Project Plan – a new task 1.4 (Send to possible contractors), which seems necessary between the original tasks 1.3 (Select contractors) and 1.4 (Review responses) and task 2.4 (Install wireless network), which was in the Project Definition, but was forgotten during the brainstorming. I have also added the whole of task 5 concerned with ensuring the new office is all working fine (and taking account of the activities to be described in Chapter 5).

Step 3.3 Estimate times, add dependencies and delays

To convert your Work Breakdown Structure into a schedule of activities, you need to add how long each task will take, and then add in any dependencies between the tasks.

Note that when a task has been broken into sub-tasks, you estimate the length of the sub-tasks and not the overall task. (The length of the overall task is a function of the lengths of the sub-tasks.) For example, as task 1 is broken into sub-tasks 1.1 to 1.6, it is each of 1.1 to 1.6 that I have estimated the length of, not task 1.

Sometimes in real life there are natural delays in activities when you have to wait for something to happen. You may be able to use this time for something else, or sometimes the project just has to wait. You need to include these delays in your plan. Examples of this include waiting for paint to dry between coats – or as in the case of our sample project, waiting for equipment that has been ordered to be delivered (see tasks 1.5, 3.3 and 4.3 in Table 3.4).

Building on the example in Table 3.3, I have added two further columns to create Table 3.4. Although this is not part of the plan, I have also included a notes column to help explain the new entries.

Task number	WBS number	Task description	Predecessor	Estimated effort (man-days)	Notes
1.	1	Select contractor to work with			See sub-tasks.
2.	1.1	Document needs (what you want the contractor to do)		0.5	
3.	1.2	Write tender (convert needs to a formal tender document)	1.1	0.5	This task can't be started until task 1.1 is complete.
4.	1.3	Select possible contractors	1.2	0.5	This task can't be started until task 1.2 is complete.
5.	1.4	Send to possible contractors	1.3	0.5	This task can't be started until task 1.3 is complete.
6.	1.5	Wait for responses	1.4	0	After ordering there will be a delay as we wait for responses. This task can't be started until task 1.4 is complete. This task has duration, but zero effort.
7.	1.6	Review responses	1.5	2	This task can't be started until task 1.5 is complete.
8.	1.7	Select contractor	1.6	1	This task can't be started until task 1.6 is complete.
9.	2	Prepare office			See sub-tasks.
10.	2.1	Design office layout	1.7	3	This task can't be started until task 1.7 is complete as we need the contractor's help.

Task number	WBS number	Task description	Predecessor	Estimated effort (man-days)	Notes
11.	2.2	Fit electrics			See sub-tasks.
12.	2.2.1	Install new lights	2.1	3	This task can't be started until task 2.1 is complete.
13.	2.2.2	Install new sockets	2.1	2	This task can't be started until task 2.1 is complete.
14.	2.3	Fit carpets	2.1	2	This task can't be started until task 2.1 is complete.
15.	2.4	Install wireless network	2.1	4	This task cannot be started until we know how the office will be laid out.
16.	3	Install furniture			See sub-tasks.
17.	3.1	Choose new furniture	1.7	1	This task can't be started until task 1.7 is complete as we want the contractor's help and advice.
18.	3.2	Order furniture	3.1	1	This task can't be started until task 3.1 is complete.
19.	3.3	Wait for furniture to be delivered	3.2	0	After ordering there is a delay as we wait for the furniture to be delivered. This task can't be started until task 3.2 is complete. This task has duration, but zero effort.
20.	3.4	Remove old furniture		1	No predecessor.

▶

Task number	WBS number	Task description	Predecessor	Estimated effort (man-days)	Notes
21.	3.5	Fit new furniture	2.3, 3.3, 3.4	2	This task can't be started until tasks 2.3, 3.3. and 3.4 are complete.
22.	4	Install new desktop equipment			See sub-tasks.
23.	4.1	Choose new docking stations		1	No predecessor.
24.	4.2	Select screens and keyboards		1	No predecessor.
25.	4.3	Order new desktop equipment	4.1, 4.2	1	This task can't be started until tasks 4.1 and 4.2 are complete.
26.	4.4	Wait for desktop equipment to be delivered	4.3	0	After ordering there will be a delay as we wait for the PCs to be delivered. This task will not start until task 4.3 is complete. This task has duration, but zero effort.
27.	4.5	Install desktop equipment	4.4	6.5	This task can't be started until task 4.4 is complete. Each docking station, screen and keyboard takes about 30 minutes to install – so a person can do 16 a day, and it will take about 6.5 days' effort to do all of them.

Task number	WBS number	Task description	Predecessor	Estimated effort (man-days)	Notes
28.	5	Test and handover			See sub tasks.
29.	5.1	Test working of wireless LAN	2.5	0.25	Critical, but not time-consuming task
30.	5.2	Allocate desks to staff	2.1	1	Although staff cannot move in until install is complete. Desks can be allocated as soon as the design is complete. To be done at a management team meeting.
31.	5.3	Wait for staff move to new office	3.5, 4.5, 5.2	0	The actual staff move is not part of this project, but an external dependency, but it still causes a delay for task 5.4. The move will not be triggered until all equipment is installed. This will take 10 days, but has zero effort from this project.
32.	5.4	Support staff as they set up at desks	5.3	2	Short-term support over first few days of moving in to make sure staff can set up correctly and everything works as planned.

Table 3.4 **Predecessors and task lengths**

Step 3.4 Add in who will do what

The next step is to allocate the tasks in the plan to the people who will do them. Nothing ever gets done unless someone does it! Each task must have the name of someone to do each task. This needs to be someone who is really and truly available to do this work.

When you first see the completed task list, you are in a position to understand what skills and what amount of resources you require.

Tasks with zero effort (such as delays), and ones that are divided into sub-tasks do not need any person allocated to them (as the project manager you will monitor these).

Task number	WBS number	Task description	Predecessor	Effort (man-days)	Who does it
1.	1	Select contractor to work with			
2.	1.1	Document needs (what you want the contractor to do)		0.5	Dave
3.	1.2	Write tender (convert needs to a formal tender document)	1.1	0.5	Dave
4.	1.3	Select possible contractors	1.2	0.5	Dave
5.	1.4	Send to possible contractors	1.3	0.5	Dave
6.	1.5	Wait for responses	1.4	0	
7.	1.6	Review responses	1.5	2	Dave
8.	1.7	Select contractor	1.6	1	Dave
9.	2	Prepare office			
10.	2.1	Design office layout	1.7	3	Contractor
11.	2.2	Fit electrics			
12.	2.2.1	Install new lights	2.1	3	Contractor
13.	2.2.2	Install new sockets	2.1	2	Contractor
14.	2.3	Fit carpets	2.1, 3.4	2	Contractor

Task number	WBS number	Task description	Predecessor	Effort (man-days)	Who does it
15.	2.4	Install wireless network	2.1	4	Adam
16.	3	Install furniture			
17.	3.1	Choose new furniture	1.6	1	Dave
18.	3.2	Order furniture	3.1	1	Dave
19.	3.3	Wait for furniture to be delivered	3.2	0	
20.	3.4	Remove old furniture		2	Contractor
21.	3.5	Fit new furniture	2.3, 3.3, 3.4	12	Contractor
22.	4	Install new desktop equipment			
23.	4.1	Choose new docking stations		1	Mary
24.	4.2	Select screens and keyboards		1	Mary
25.	4.3	Order new desktop equipment	4.1, 4.2	1	Mary
26.	4.4	Wait for desktop equipment to be delivered		0	
27.	4.5	Install desktop equipment	4.4	6.5	Contractor
28.	5	Test and handover			
29.	5.1	Test working of wireless LAN	2.5	0.25	Adam
30.	5.2	Allocate desks to staff	2.1	0.5	Dave + management team
31.	5.3	Wait for staff move to new office	3.5, 4.5, 5.2	10	
32.	5.4	Support staff as they set up at desks	5.3	2	Mary

Table 3.5 **Task allocation**

Step 3.5 Build the plan into a schedule

The schedule is the start and end dates for each task, and from that the start and end date for the overall project. The end date is simply the start date plus the effort (in reality it is a bit more complex than this – but this will do for now). The start date is determined by:

- When any predecessor tasks are finished (and do not forget external dependencies).

- When the people who are to do this task have completed previous steps they are allocated to work on.

- When the people who do this task are available (i.e. not weekends, not holidays, not doing other non-project work). This is easiest if everyone is 100 per cent on the project (see the end of this section for further points on this).

Building on the example in Table 3.5, I have added two further columns to give Table 3.6. I have used a 2016 calendar and UK public holidays to work out dates and to exclude weekends and bank holidays. Although this is not part of the plan, I have also included a notes column to help explain the new entries.

Task number	WBS number	Task description	Predecessor	Effort (Delay)	Who does it	Start	End	Notes
1.	1	Select contractor to work with						See sub-tasks
2.	1.1	Document needs (what you want the contractor to do)		0.5	Dave	31 May	31 May	Project starts on Tuesday 31 May. (Monday 30 2016 is a public holiday in the UK)
3.	1.2	Write tender (convert needs to a formal tender document)	1.1	0.5	Dave	31 May	31 May	1.1 + 0.5 days
4.	1.3	Select possible contractors	1.2	0.5	Dave	1 June	1 June	1.2 + 0.5 days
5.	1.4	Send to possible contractors	1.3	0.5	Dave	1 June	1 June	1.3 + 0.5 days
6.	1.5	Wait for responses	1.4	+10	Delay	2 June	15 June	1.4 + 10 days (Delay 10 working = 2 calendar weeks)
7.	1.6	Review responses	1.5	2	Dave	16 June	17 June	1.5 + 2 days
8.	1.7	Select contractor	1.6	1	Dave	20 June	20 June	1.6 + 1 day. Select contractor who can start immediately

▶

Task number	WBS number	Task description	Predecessor	Effort (Delay)	Who does it	Start	End	Notes
9.	2	Prepare office						See sub-tasks
10.	2.1	Design office layout	1.7	3	Contractor	21 June	23 June	1.7 + 3 days
11.	2.2	Fit electrics						See sub-tasks
12.	2.2.1	Install new lights	2.1	3	Contractor	24 June	28 June	2.1 + 3 days
13.	2.2.2	Install new sockets	2.1	2	Contractor	29 June	30 June	2.2.1 + 2 days (Predecessor is 2.1, but contractor won't be available until completed 2.2.1)
14.	2.3	Fit carpets	2.1, 3.4	2	Contractor	7 July	8 July	Latest of 2.1 and 3.4 + 2 days
15.	2.4	Install wireless network	2.1	4	Adam	24 June	29 June	2.1 + 4 days (can probably be started later without causing a problem)
16.	3	Install furniture						See sub-tasks
17.	3.1	Choose new furniture	1.7	2	Dave	21 June	22 June	1.7 + 2 days
18.	3.2	Order furniture	3.1	1	Dave	23 June	23 June	3.1 + 1 day
19.	3.3	Wait for furniture to be delivered	3.2	+20	Delay	24 June	21 July	3.2 + 20 days

STEP 3: CREATE YOUR PROJECT PLAN

#	ID	Task	Predecessor	Duration	Resource	Start	End	Notes
20.	3.4	Remove old furniture		4	Contractor	1 July	6 July	No predecessor, but contractor not available until completed 2.2.2
21.	3.5	Fit new furniture	2.3, 3.3, 3.4	12	Contractor	22 July	8 Aug	Latest of 2.3, 3.3 and 3.4 + 12 days
22.	4	Install new desktop equipment						See sub-tasks
23.	4.1	Choose new docking stations		2	Mary	31 May	1 June	No predecessor, can start when project starts
24.	4.2	Select screens and keyboards		2	Mary	2 June	3 June	No predecessor, can start when project starts, but Mary not available until she has completed 4.1
25.	4.3	Order new desktop equipment	4.1, 4.2	1	Mary	6 June	6 June	4.2 + 1 day
26.	4.4	Wait for desktop equipment to be delivered	4.3	+20	Delay	7 June	4 July	4.3 + 20 days
27.	4.5	Install desktop equipment	3.5, 4.4	6.5	Mary	9 Aug	17 Aug	Latest of 3.5 or 4.4 + 6.5 days
28.	5	Test and handover						

▶

Task number	WBS number	Task description	Predecessor	Effort (Delay)	Who does it	Start	End	Notes
29.	5.1	Test working of wireless LAN	2.4	0.25	Adam	30 July	30 July	2.4 + 0.25 days
30.	5.2	Allocate desks to staff	2.1, Management team meeting	0.5	Dave + management team	4 July	4 July	Date fixed by time of next management team meeting on the first Monday of the month after task 2.1
31.	5.3	Wait for staff move to new office	3.5, 4.5, 5.2	+10	Delay	18 Aug	1 Sep	Latest of 2.1, 3.5, 4.5 and 5.2 +10 days
32.	5.4	Support staff as they set up at desks	5.3	2	Mary	2 Sep	5 Sep	5.3 + 2 days

Table 3.6 **Predecessors and task lengths**

The dates in the schedule measure elapsed time or duration – and not effort. Therefore don't forget when you are working out times:

- Weekends are normally to be excluded, (e.g. 10 working days is two calendar weeks).

- Public holidays are normally excluded. (On this schedule 30 May and 29 August are excluded as 2016 UK public holidays.)

- You need to account for personal holidays. If Mary has two weeks' holiday starting on 15 August, task 5.4 will have delay in the middle of it or someone else will have to be allocated. (In this plan no holidays have been assumed.)

- People may be working on other things at the same time. Often people are not available 100 per cent of the time. So if Mary is not only doing your project, but must also give 50 per cent of her time to another project, all the elapsed times for tasks she is responsible for will need to be doubled. For example, an effort of two days will take four elapsed days for someone 50 per cent available. I have assumed 100 per cent availability.

- Remember to consider how many days a week people are ever available. In practice, no one is available for five days a week for anything more than a short period of time. People always have other things to do at work, have days off and are sick from time to time. On a very short project, when you involve someone for a week or two, it is fair to assume you will get 100 per cent of their focus. How much time you get from someone does depend on their job and what other activities they need to do. A good rule of thumb is that you will get 4½ productive days a week from someone accounting for other things they need to do. (Add up the time you spend handling your calls, emails, having coffee, in meetings or walking around the office – let alone training and holidays, etc.)

- In this case study I have assumed that when there are delays, the project does not have to pay for people's time as they have other projects to work on. This will not always be true.

- The timing of task 5.2 depends on an external dependency on a management team meeting. Such decision points in projects, whose timing is dependent on regular management or leadership meetings, are common and they often extend the duration of the project.

This is really where planning software comes into its own. It will automatically calculate the start and end dates, and change them immediately you change the length of any other task, or the availability of people to do the work. It can speed up the process of creating a plan and remove a lot of hassle. When used, planning software removes an administrative burden but the end plan will not be better because you used it.

Step 3.6 Work out costs

To work out the costs you must identify the cost elements from the project as shown in Table 3.7. Remember the elements of cost are:

- Costs associated with running the project. These include the time of people working on the project and anything you must buy to enable them to complete their work. Do not forget that your time as the project manager needs to be included, even though this is not shown as a task on the plan.

- Costs associated with buying deliverables, or anything used to create your deliverables on the project.

PROJECT BUDGET	Project name:	Office re-fit project		
Project staff costs (variable)				Totals
Person	Unit cost	Units	Total	
Dave	£400 per day	9.5 days	£3,800	
Mary	£500 per day	11.5 days	£5,750	
Adam	£440 per day	4.5 days	£1,980	
Project Manager	£450 per day	70 days	£31,500	
	Total project staff costs		£43,030	
Other project variable costs				
Item	Unit cost	Units	Total	
Office rental	£1,000 per week	13 weeks	£13,000	
	Total project variable costs		£13,000	

Project fixed costs				Totals
Item			Total item cost	
Contractor (set fee)			£20,000	
Copy of project management software			£400	
Total project fixed costs			£20,400	
Total cost to run project				£76,430
Deliverable variable costs				
Item	Unit cost	Units	Total	
Chairs	£100 per chair	100	£10,000	
Desks	£300 per desk	100	£30,000	
Docking station, screen and keyboard	£300 per laptop	100	£30,000	
Light fittings	£150 per light	40	£6,000	
Socket fittings	£75 per socket	200	£15,000	
Carpet	£50 per m2	1250	£50,000	
Total deliverable variable costs			£141,000	
Deliverable fixed costs				
Item			Total item cost	
Miscellaneous additional furniture			£10,000	
Wireless LAN, cabling and routers			£5,000	
Disposal of old furniture and carpets			£5,000	
Total deliverable fixed costs			£20,000	
Total costs for project deliverables				£161,000
Total project budget required				£237,430

Table 3.7 Project costs

Step 3.7 Add in milestones and contingency

Put in milestones that give some key dates and that will help communicate and explain the plan to your customer, and which you can use as overall markers of progress. To select milestones, choose key events that are meaningful and helpful to your customer. The milestones for this chapter's example could be:

- 8 July – Office fitted and ready to furnish (at completion of task 2.3)

- 17 August – Office ready (at completion of task 4.5)

- 5 September – Project complete (at completion of task 5.4)

You add contingency to account for the inherent risk in the project. This can be done in two ways:

1. *As a top-down estimate.* Looking at the whole plan and using a feel for how much risk there is. This is effectively a project manager's intuition, or gut-feel, about the project. The example project feels like a reasonably low-risk project to me, so I would add a 10–20 per cent buffer to costs and time.

2. *As a bottom-up estimate.* Looking at every individual task in the plan and identifying how much risk there is associated with every time and cost estimate. This is where you look at the individual elements of the project and identify risks and add contingency for each of them. This is generally more accurate, but can be very time-consuming for a complex project because you may have hundreds of tasks to review. For the example project, this is what I have done.

So what are the riskiest parts of this plan? From my perspective I think they are:

- The assumption that the project manager starts on day one of the project plan. Usually you need the project manager before this, as they create the plan. Add five days of fees for the project manager prior to the plan start (£2,250).

- The assumption that your contractor will be ready to start work the day after you have selected him or her. Allow 10 days' contingency here.

- The delays waiting for equipment and furniture to be delivered. What if your suppliers are late? Allow another 10 days' contingency here.

- The deliverable variable costs. You know the costs of desktop equipment, but the furniture and fitting costs are best guesses and could be wrong. Allow an extra 10 per cent budget for these items – or £14,100 (10 per cent of £141,000).

- The cost of staff required if you use the 10 days' contingency. Most of the 10 days' contingency if used will be extra waiting time when no one is working, but it may add 20 days to the project manager's time (£9,000), some extra days for Dave managing getting the contractor on board (£800).

There is no great science to the estimates I have used for contingency, other than that they seem about right. There are more formal approaches and algorithms you can use for calculating contingency, but unless the project is complex these are unnecessary. Where you know you can estimate something accurately, you need little contingency. Where you do not know, or there are many assumptions about a task, you must add more. You are the project manager. It is your project. You must add enough contingency to give yourself confidence you can deliver the project.

Having contingency does not mean that you give the people doing those tasks an extra 20 days and £26,150 to spend. The project manager holds this as a buffer you can use only when you need to. We will explore this more in Chapter 4. What this means though is that you will ask:

- For a project budget of £263,580 (budget + contingency), I would round up to a budget of £265k.

- For time to complete until 3 October.

Does adding an additional 20 days seem a lot? That can only be decided when you know the impact of getting the project duration wrong. What if you made all staff leave their existing office when the project is meant to complete and terminated your current rental from that date? If you tell everyone you will complete on 5 September and are not ready, there's a big problem for your business. Where then will the business work from? Better have some contingency and avoid this risk. You may even decide that, given the business risk, 20 days is not enough contingency. Now is the time to be sensibly cautious, not heroically overoptimistic.

Step 3.8 Review and amend – can you do it, should you do it, is there a better way?

You have a plan, and you have an understanding of the budget you require to deliver this plan. Before you move on to starting to deliver the project, there are three related questions to ask yourself:

1. *Can you do it?* The project you have planned will take just over four months (31 May to 7 October), cost you £265k, and requires

the time of Mary, Dave, Adam and a contractor. Do you actually have this time and money and access to these people?

2. ***Should you do it?*** Going back to your original reason for your project, will the plan you have developed meet it? For example, if you are moving office to reduce your office rental by £500k per annum, then you will probably think spending £265k to achieve this is a good investment. However, if your saving is only £50k per annum then £265k is probably too much to spend to save this amount, and the project is not worth doing. The planning was still a worthwhile activity as it proved this.

3. ***Can you do it any better way?*** Your plan is just one way of doing the work: is there any way you can juggle the plan to do it faster, cheaper or better? You do not need to look at everything, but by exploring the key items in cost and the things that make the timeline as long as it is, you may find things you can cut. Look at how you can juggle between the five dimensions of the project: time, cost, scope, quality and risk.

In the project example, the major costs are the deliverable variable costs – buying the furniture and desktop equipment for your staff. If you need to reduce costs, can you buy cheaper desktop equipment or cheaper furniture? Don't forget the quality you need, but these form almost half the cost of your project, so savings here will help.

You should also review the time your plan shows the project taking. To do this there is one useful piece of project management jargon to understand, that is the critical path of a project.

The critical path is the series of tasks that create the timescale of the project. Other tasks that are not on the critical path can move around without changing the overall length of the project, unless they are changed so much as to become the critical path.

You can work out the critical path by starting with the last task in the project to finish and working backwards through the plan to identify the tasks that determine this date. In the office re-fit project, the critical path is shown by the highlighted task number, the predecessor that creates the critical path in bold and task details in italic (see Table 3.8). If you start at task 5.4 you can trace the critical path backwards. To shorten the project you need to shorten one or more of these tasks.

Task number	WBS number	Task description	Predecessor	Effort/Delay	Who does it	Start	End
1.	1	Select contractor to work with					
2.	1.1	Document needs (what you want the contractor to do)		0.5	Dave	31 May	31 May
3.	1.2	Write tender (convert needs to a formal tender document)	1.1	0.5	Dave	31 May	31 May
4.	1.3	Select possible contractors	1.2	0.5	Dave	1 June	1 June
5.	1.4	Send to possible contractors	1.3	0.5	Dave	1 June	1 June
6.	1.5	Wait for responses	1.4	+10	Delay	2 June	15 June
7.	1.6	Review responses	1.5	2	Dave	16 June	17 June
8.	1.7	Select contractor	1.6	1	Dave	20 June	20 June
9.	2	Prepare office					
10.	2.1	Design office layout	1.7	3	Contractor	21 June	23 June
11.	2.2	Fit electrics					
12.	2.2.1	Install new lights	2.1	3	Contractor	24 June	28 June
13.	2.2.2	Install new sockets	2.1	2	Contractor	29 June	30 June
14.	2.3	Fit carpets	2.1, 3.4	2	Contractor	7 July	8 July
15.	2.4	Install wireless network	2.1	4	Adam	24 June	29 June
16.	3	Install furniture					
17.	3.1	Choose new furniture	1.7	2	Dave	21 June	22 June
18.	3.2	Order furniture	3.1	1	Dave	23 June	23 June

▶

85

Task number	WBS number	Task description	Predecessor	Effort/Delay	Who does it	Start	End
19.	3.3	Wait for furniture to be delivered	3.2	+20	Delay	24 June	21 July
20.	3.4	Remove old furniture		4	Contractor	1 July	6 July
21.	3.5	Fit new furniture	2.3, 3.3, 3.4	12	Contractor	22 July	8 Aug
22.	4	Install new desktop equipment					
23.	4.1	Choose new docking stations		2	Mary	31 May	1 June
24.	4.2	Select screens and keyboards		2	Mary	2 June	3 June
25.	4.3	Order new desktop equipment	4.1, 4.2	1	Mary	6 June	6 June
26.	4.4	Wait for desktop equipment to be delivered	4.3	+20	Delay	7 June	4 July
27.	4.5	Install desktop equipment	3.5, 4.4	6.5	Mary	9 Aug	17 Aug
28.	5	Test and handover					
29.	5.1	Test working of wireless LAN	2.4	0.25	Adam	30 July	30 July
30.	5.2	Allocate desks to staff	2.1, Management team meeting	0.5	Dave + management team	4 July	4 July
31.	5.3	Wait for staff move to new office	3.5, 4.5, 5.2	+10	Delay	18 Aug	1 Sep
32.	5.4	Support staff as they set up at desks	5.3	2	Mary	2 Sep	5 Sep

Table 3.8 The critical path

If any of the dates in italic move, then the whole project timeline will change. For example, if task 1.1 (Document needs) or 1.2 (Write tender) are one day late in completing, then the whole project will be one day late and slip from 5 September to 6 September. In comparison, task 4.4 (Wait for desktop equipment to be delivered) can slip by five weeks without changing the overall end date.

For you to improve on the timeline of the project there are various factors to consider:

- *Can you remove any of the tasks?* In this example, there are lights already in the offices and although they are not perfect, they are good enough and can be changed later on. This will remove task 2.2.1 (Install new lights), and so save £6,000 of cost and reduce the contractor's work by three days.

- *Are estimates reasonable or can they be reduced?* This is an obvious concept to explore, and if you challenge estimates you will find that some are longer than they need to be. However, if you are too aggressive in challenging people, you may get shorter times in the plan, but they will be unrealistic.

- *Can you remove any dependency?* For example, if task 4.6 (Install desktop equipment) was not dependent on task 3.5 (Fit new furniture) you could start it on 5 July rather than 9 August. This is over a month earlier and would allow you to complete the project a month earlier too. Unfortunately, in this case you cannot. But check all dependencies as sometimes you will find they are not correct. Professional project managers always try to reduce dependencies to only those essential.

- *Can you overlap any tasks?* Task 4.5 (Install desktop equipment) may require 3.5 (Fit new furniture) to be started as you need desks to install the equipment on. But you don't need it to be finished, as you only need one desk to be installed to fit the first set of equipment. This means 4.5 must start after 3.5, but only so enough desks are completed to put the desktop equipment on. If you start 4.5 after two days of desk installation, it will start 10 days earlier than in the current plan, and the overall plan will be shortened.

● *Can you use any of the resources more efficiently?* The best way to do this is to look again at the plan. In the plan the tasks are ordered by WBS number. Re-sort the plan to order the tasks by who is doing them, followed by the date each task starts, as shown in Table 3.9.

Task number	WBS number	Task description	Predecessor	Effort	Who does it	Start	End
15.	2.4	Install wireless network	2.1	4	**Adam**	24 June	29 June
29.	5.1	Test working of wireless LAN	2.4	0.25	Adam	30 July	30 July
10.	2.1	Design office layout	1.7	3	**Contractor**	21 June	23 June
12.	2.2.1	Install new lights	2.1	3	Contractor	24 June	28 June
13.	2.2.2	Install new sockets	2.1	2	Contractor	29 June	30 June
14.	2.3	Fit carpets	2.1, 3.4	2	Contractor	7 July	8 July
20.	3.4	Remove old furniture		4	Contractor	1 July	6 July
21.	3.5	Fit new furniture	2.3, 3.3, 3.4	12	Contractor	22 July	8 Aug
2.	1.1	Document needs (what you want the contractor to do)		0.5	**Dave**	31 May	31 May
3.	1.2	Write tender (convert needs to a formal tender document)	1.1	0.5	Dave	31 May	31 May
4.	1.3	Select possible contractors	1.2	0.5	Dave	1 June	1 June
5.	1.4	Send to possible contractors	1.3	0.5	Dave	1 June	1 June
7.	1.6	Review responses	1.5	2	Dave	16 June	17 June

▶

Task number	WBS number	Task description	Predecessor	Effort	Who does it	Start	End
8.	1.7	Select contractor	1.6	1	Dave	20 June	20 June
17.	3.1	Choose new furniture	1.7	2	Dave	21 June	22 June
18.	3.2	Order furniture	3.1	1	Dave	23 June	23 June
30.	5.2	Allocate desks to staff	2.1, Management team meeting	0.5	Dave + management team	4 July	4 July
23.	4.1	Choose new docking stations		2	**Mary**	31 May	1 June
24.	4.2	Select screens and keyboards		2	Mary	2 June	3 June
25.	4.3	Order new desktop equipment	4.1, 4.2	1	Mary	6 June	6 June
27.	4.5	Install desktop equipment	3.5, 4.4	6.5	Mary	9 Aug	17 Aug
28.	5	Test and handover					
32.	5.4	Support staff as they set up at desks	5.3	2	Mary	2 Sep	5 Sep

Table 3.9 Plan sorted by person

If you analyse the work of each individual member of the project team (Adam, the contractor, Dave and Mary) in Table 3.9, you can determine that:

- Adam has only two tasks to do on the plan which are roughly a month apart. They could be done without a gap, and can be done at any time prior to staff moving in.

- The contractor is involved in the project from 21 June to 8 August, but doing nothing for 10 working days between 8 and 22 July.

- Dave is involved on the project from 31 May to 4 July, but doing nothing between tasks 1.4 and 1.5, and between tasks 3.2 and 5.2. Dave has no work to do on the project for 15 days of the elapsed time on the project.

- Mary is involved on the project from 31 May to 5 September, but has long gaps when she is not required between 6 June to 9 August, and 17 August to 2 September.

You want everyone in the project team to be busy all the time they are on the project if you are paying for their time. To achieve this you may need to move some tasks around. For Dave and the contractor it is difficult to see any way to easily reorganise the plan so these gaps do not exist. However, by warning them in advance, you could:

- Find other work for you that is not related to your project.

- Expand the scope of the project and get them to do something additional during their free days.

- Agree with them that they are not working for you on those days.

You should look at rescheduling for efficiency as well. Mary needs to be involved until the end of the project, 5 September. However, tasks 4.1 to 4.3 are not on the critical path. They can be moved to make more efficient scheduling of her time. Originally, she was due to start task 4.1 on the earliest date she could, i.e. 31 May. Alternatively, she could start work as late as the 5 July without impacting the overall project schedule.

Can you add in more resource? Would any of the tasks be completed faster if more people were to work on them? Not all tasks are capable of being split amongst people. Yet it seems reasonable to assume that if tasks 3.5 (Fit new furniture), 4.5 (Install new desktop equipment) had twice as many people working on them, they could be done twice as fast.

If you make all these changes, your final plan looks like Table 3.10.

PROJECT PLAN	Project name:	Office re-fit plan					
Task number	WBS number	Task description	Predecessors	Effort (delay)	Who does it	Start	End
1.	*1*	*Select contractor to work with*					
2.	1.1	Document needs (what you want the contractor to do)		0.5	Dave	31 May	31 May
3.	1.2	Write tender (convert needs to a formal tender document)	1.1	0.5	Dave	31 May	31 May
4.	1.3	Select possible contractors	1.2	0.5	Dave	1 June	1 June
5.	1.4	Send to possible contractors	1.3	0.5	Dave	1 June	1 June
6.	1.5	Wait for responses	1.4	+10	Delay	2 June	15 June
7.	1.6	Review responses	1.5	2	Dave	16 June	17 June
8.	1.7	Select contractor	1.6	1	Dave	20 June	20 June
9.	*2*	*Prepare office*					
10.	2.1	Design office layout	1.7	3	Contractor	21 June	23 June
11.	2.2	Fit electrics					
12.	2.2.1	Install new lights	2.1	3	Contractor	24 June	28 June
13.	2.2.2	Install new sockets	2.1	2	Contractor	29 June	30 June
14.	2.3	Fit carpets	2.1, 3.4	2	Contractor	7 July	8 July

PROJECT PLAN	Project name:	Office re-fit plan					
Task number	WBS number	Task description	Predecessors	Effort (delay)	Who does it	Start	End
15.		MILESTONE 1: Office live					8 July
16.	2.4	Install wireless network	2.1	4	Adam	25 July	29 July
17.	*3*	*Install furniture*					
18.	3.1	Choose new furniture	1.7	2	Dave	21 June	22 June
19.	3.2	Order furniture	3.1	1	Dave	23 June	23 June
20.	3.3	Wait for furniture to be delivered	3.2	+20	Delay	24 June	21 July
21.	3.4	Remove old furniture		4	Contractor	1 July	6 July
22.	3.5	Fit new furniture	2.3, 3.3, 3.4	12	Contractor	22 July	8 Aug
23.	*4*	*Install new desktop equipment*					
24.	4.1	Choose new docking stations		2	Mary	5 July	6 July
25.	4.2	Select screens and keyboards		2	Mary	7 July	8 July
26.	4.3	Order new desktop equipment	4.1, 4.2	1	Mary	11 July	11 July
27.	4.4	Wait for desktop equipment to be delivered	4.3	+20	Delay	12 July	8 July
28.	4.5	Install desktop equipment	3.5, 4.4	6.5	Mary	9 Aug	17 Aug
29.		MILESTONE 2: Office ready for use					17 Aug

30.	**5**	***Test and handover***						
31.	5.1	Test working of wireless LAN	2.4	0.25	Adam	30 July	30 July	30 July
32.	5.2	Allocate desks to staff	2.1, Management team meeting	0.5	Dave + management team	4 July	4 July	4 July
33.	5.3	Wait for staff move to new office	3.5, 4.5, 5.2	+10	Delay	18 Aug	1 Sep	
34.	5.4	Support staff as they set up at desks	5.3	2	Mary	2 Sep	5 Sep	
35.			**MILESTONE 3: Project complete**				**5 Sep**	
36.	*Contingency*			20	Project Manager	6 Sep	3 Oct	
37.			**Committed project completion date**				**3 Oct**	

Table 3.10 **The Project Plan**

Now you have a plan and are ready to start your project!

Step 3.9 Review the plan with your project customer

The final activity for you to do is to explain your plan to your project customer. The key information they will probably be interested in is the time and cost of your project. Once they understand this and accept it, you will move on to the next step – delivering your project.

When your customer reviews the plan, there are typically two challenges they may give you, which you should avoid. Your customer may well ask for:

- **_The project to be done more quickly and cheaply._** Resist the temptation to agree to this; you now know much more about the plan than they do. If they have a great idea as to how to achieve the reduction in time or cost, then fine. But generally, if the project customer wants the project done more quickly or cheaply, then something else has to change. Perhaps you can reduce the scope or quality of deliverables – if not, then the plan must stay as it is.

- **_The contingency to be removed._** Your customer may think that if the project is planned properly, you do not really need the contingency. You know you need it, but it can be difficult to justify. The way you justify it depends on the relationship with your customer, but you have three main choices:

  - Try to convince them the contingency is essential. This is the best way, but it is not always possible. Consider the contingency as an insurance premium.

  - Show them only the milestones. Do not explain the detailed plan, but only explain high-level milestones. In the example used in the chapter, the project completion is shown as 3 October. If you deliver on 5 September and save them some money they will be very happy!

  - Hide the contingency by padding out other tasks. This is not a good way of managing work although it is often what project managers do.

- If they really insist on analysing the plan and removing the contingency get the customer to accept the risk.

Whatever you do, do not fall for the trap of taking out the contingency!

Key drivers for success 4 — Manage expectations

When you start your project and have agreed the overall Project Plan with your customer, you have set an expectation with them that the work will be complete in a certain time and to a certain budget. As you go through the project anything might happen to stop you achieving this – perhaps your plan is wrong, perhaps some issues arise which you have not foreseen, or perhaps the customer asks for some change which extends the project.

Whatever causes the project to change, it is best to make sure your customer understands this as soon as possible. If you think your project will be late or over budget, tell your customer as soon as you know, and do not wait for the end of the project for this to be a surprise to them. You must manage their expectations *so that what happens is what the customer expects.*

To manage expectations, you have to really understand what is happening on the project. You cannot stop customer surprises if you are getting surprised yourself!

When you go to the garage to have your car fixed, you may want it done in one day but sometimes the garage cannot do this. Isn't it better when they tell you at the start that the car will take three days to fix, rather than you turn up at the end of the first day only to be told to come back later? Similarly, if when fixing your car the garage finds a further problem which will take them an extra couple of days to fix, don't you want them to call you and tell you – or would you prefer to turn up again and be told, 'Oh sorry, it's not ready, come back in two days' time'? Most people like to know in advance if there will be a delay or an unexpected increase in cost.

Great project managers know that managing expectations is the key to keeping your customers happy – and a happy customer is a sign of success.

Key tips

- Resist the pressure to skimp on planning so you can start the work immediately. What time you spend up-front on planning will be repaid several times over in time saved later.

- Understand the difference between the effort an activity takes and the duration of it.

- Contingency is not poor management, but a realistic and essential component of a plan to account for the risk inherent in any task.

- Focus on getting your plan complete more than worrying about estimates. A poor estimate will mean you may overrun on time, but a missed task may mean you cannot complete the work. (Read Chapter 5 for some important tasks that are easy to forget at planning time.)

- Get the right team, as no matter how good a plan you have, without the right project team the work will not get done.

- Planning software helps you present and manage your plan, it does not ensure your plan is any better.

TO DO NOW

- Start getting ready to brainstorm a task list:

  - Where are you going to do it?

  - When are you going to do it?

  - Who are you going to work with? Do they offer the best combination of common sense and experience of this type of work? Have you got the time booked in their diaries?

- Having completed the brainstorm, continue to follow each element of this step. Continually ask yourself, do you believe the plan you are developing?

Taking it further: Using external contractors and companies

In many projects, including the example shown in this chapter, you may end up using staff who do not work for your business as part of the project team. The use of contractors, consultants and third-party suppliers is common. These external contractors may have specialist skills, provide some service you do not know how to do yourself, or may simply be an additional resource to get over any shortages you have while running the project.

For individual contractors, you should manage them as you would any other member of the project team. There are many advantages and disadvantages of using a contractor compared to a colleague who works for the same business as you. As the project manager, you generally have a little more leverage over them than employees. If they do not deliver what you have employed them to do, you may not pay them or may choose to replace them with a different contractor.

An alternative scenario with an external company working on your project is where they take total responsibility for a section of the project and they manage it themselves. If you do this your project management task can become a lot simpler, as what was a whole series of complex tasks on your plan may become a single task with a start and end date, the details of which are invisible to you. This 'black box' type of task has many attractions. For one thing, you don't need to worry about who is doing something or how they do it – only the start and end date and the cost. For this to work well you really have to trust your third-party supplier. Care is needed as they are often just as likely to be late as you would have been if doing it yourself. You need confidence that they have some capability or resources which you don't that enable them to deliver more reliably than you would on your own.

If you do choose to use a third-party supplier to be responsible for a whole section of the plan, then they must plan this task themselves. When they tell you how long they will take and how much they will charge you should:

- At least challenge their timelines and costs: ask why can't it be done cheaper or quicker? You will often find that with some respectful but demanding challenges a supplier can deliver more quickly and more cheaply.

- Ask to see their plan, so you can at least check that they have one. If they do not, you should not be confident in their ability to do your work, unless the task is quite simple.

- Make them put some periodic milestones in their plans which are visible to you. This will give you confidence that their work is on track as the project progresses – or at least it will forewarn you if it is not.

FURTHER READING

- **Contractors and consultants:** Newton, R., *The Management Consultant: Mastering the Art of Consultancy*, FT Prentice Hall, 2010

Step 4

Manage delivery

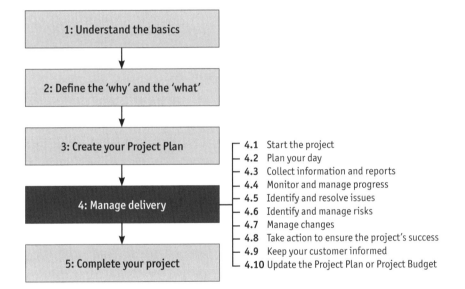

1: Understand the basics	

2: Define the 'why' and the 'what'	

3: Create your Project Plan	4.1 Start the project
	4.2 Plan your day
	4.3 Collect information and reports
	4.4 Monitor and manage progress
4: Manage delivery	4.5 Identify and resolve issues
	4.6 Identify and manage risks
	4.7 Manage changes
	4.8 Take action to ensure the project's success
5: Complete your project	4.9 Keep your customer informed
	4.10 Update the Project Plan or Project Budget

THIS CHAPTER COVERS:

- The day-to-day work of the project manager on an active project.

To ensure that all the different considerations in managing a project are covered, the detailed example used in Chapter 3 is continued. When you have completed this chapter you will understand most of the work of the project manager.

THE CENTRAL POINT IS:

- Projects need to be actively managed to ensure they are successfully delivered. There is a straightforward set of management tasks a project manager has to undertake throughout the life of a project, to ensure the smooth progress of the project.

Setting the scene

In the rest of this chapter I continue with the example of the office move project started in Chapter 3. To set the scene, and to show different ways the project approach can be used, I am going to briefly use a different example, this time of organising a conference. This example is used as they are easy to understand, and therefore you can focus on understanding the project management processes and tools rather than trying to understand the project itself.

Imagine you have been asked to set up a series of conferences. You have a good understanding of what is wanted. You must organise four big conferences with several hundred people at each, who all should be looked after throughout the three days of every conference. Speakers and presenters need to be identified and invited. Marketing materials must be developed and distributed. Attendees have to be contacted, invited and fees collected from them. You want the conferences to be sponsored by large corporations. The conference centres themselves need to be identified, booked and set up specifically for your requirements. Travel, catering and accommodation need to be arranged for everyone. All in all this is a complex activity, which will require several people to work on for some period of time to achieve the objective; in other words, it is a *project*.

You develop a well-structured Project Plan and identify who will do all the work to arrange the conferences. Can't you now just sit back and let this project happen according to the plan?

Unfortunately, the answer is no. Things do not happen by themselves. When you have a plan describing how to do a project, the work still needs to be explicitly allocated and explained to people. No one will book the conference venues unless they are asked to. Even when you have a project team who understand the plan and their role on it, they may not reliably get it all done. People have lots of things to do apart from your project, and will not automatically keep their attention on it. Your project team members may be working on one or two other projects as well, and unless you keep them focused, they may not do the work to arrange your conferences quickly enough. As they work on your project, problems will arise. These problems, if they are not resolved, will cause progress to be interrupted. For instance, one of the key members of your project team may become ill and not be able to work over a critical period in the project. To make matters worse, customers have a tendency to decide halfway through a project that they want something different from what they originally asked for – perhaps your customer decides that rather than four conferences of three days each, it is better to have three conferences of four days each. Such a decision will throw your work into disarray. For these reasons, and many more, projects do not just happen, they need to be led, managed and directed, and this is the role of the project manager.

Introduction to the role of the project manager

Having reached this stage in the book, you are in an excellent position to deliver your project successfully. You clearly understand why you are doing the project, what it will deliver, and how you will deliver this.

The goal you must now strive to achieve is to deliver your project predictably to the defined scope, quality, time, cost and level of risk. Everything you have done up to this point will help this – now you must make it happen. To achieve this you need to:

- Ensure that the project is started properly, and that each project team member understands their role and what tasks they need to do.

- Manage progress and ensure day to day that the work on the project is moving along as you have planned.

- Resolve any problems that are getting in the way of progress.

- Look out for things in the future that may get in the way of progress, which you can avoid by taking action now.

● Make certain that the project objectives remain relevant to your customer, and where they do not, change the project in a controlled way.

Apart from starting the project, these tasks are not one-off activities, but a continuous set of work for the project manager through the life of the project. On a small project such tasks will not keep you 100 per cent busy and you will have time to do other things. On larger projects the role of the project manager is a full-time one.

To be effective as a project manager you must keep yourself immersed in the day-to-day work of the project and understand what is happening. You need to keep talking all the time to the project team, telling them what needs to be done and finding out how they are progressing. Project management is not a hands-off activity, it requires focus, attention and ongoing interaction with everyone involved in the project.

Before I define how to perform these tasks on a live project I explain the key items you must manage, and introduce four pieces of useful project management jargon:

● Progress

● Issues

● Risks

● Changes.

Measuring and managing progress on a project

The most important task for the project manager is to manage progress – ensuring the project is progressing quickly enough to deliver the desired end result in the timeframe wanted without spending more money than was expected.

Managing progress is about ensuring that the pace of work being done by yourself and other project team members is matching that planned and required. To be able to determine this, you must have a way of measuring progress. Because you have a plan, you have something to measure with. One way to think of the plan, is as a project manager's measuring device. However, a plan is simply a view of how the future might work, it is not a statement of reality and no project ever goes exactly to plan. The plan provides a baseline for the project manager to assess whether things are going fast enough or not – and if they are not, to take action to speed them up again. Consider a single task on a plan:

- If the task has a start date of 1 September and is allocated to David, then by 1 September David should be working on that task, or else the project will start to become late.

- If the same task is due to be complete by 15 September, unless it is 100 per cent complete by 15 September, your project is becoming late.

In both cases, if you want the project to stay on time you must take some action to get the task completed on time. Remember though, when you developed your plan, you put in the reasonable time to complete a task – not the maximum, so you are almost certain to run late on some tasks. Running late in itself is not a problem, and you should expect it to happen now and again. But you need to know that it is happening, decide what to do about it, and implement the action you have decided upon.

The key to measuring progress is to understand that progress is about *completing* tasks, and not just working on them. Just because you are five days into a 10-day task does not mean you are halfway through it, it simply means half your time is used up. From a project manager's perspective, being halfway through a task means you have completed half the work that needs to be done. It is often very difficult to assess quite how much of a task has been done. If there is no easy way to measure progress, the simple rule of thumb is that a task is either 0 per cent complete, or it is 100 per cent complete and finished. You should only accept that tasks are complete when they are 100 per cent complete.

To measure progress, you must collect information on how much work people have done. While it is good to trust people, as the project manager you don't just want people to say they have done tasks, you should ask for evidence. If a project team member is meant to have produced a report, ask to see it. If a project team member is meant to have done some market research, ask him to show you the results. If a project team member is meant to have ordered 50 smartphones, ask her to confirm when they will be delivered. If a project team member is meant to have thought about and planned some work, ask to see the plan. Some tasks create an easily identifiable physical deliverable while others do not, but even those that do not usually produce something which can be measured indirectly or have some impact that can be assessed.

Consider the situation in which one of the tasks requires a team member to meet and interview a specialist for advice. For evidence, ask to see the meeting minutes or notes. Perhaps a task requires a project team member to motivate some staff: for evidence, talk to the staff yourself – do they seem more motivated?

Once you have a view of the work completed, you can check this against the plan to see if you have made as much progress as planned. You should check two main things:

1. That you are progressing at least as fast as you planned.

2. That you are spending your budget no faster than you planned.

There are two ways of looking at the rates of work being done and money being spent:

- ***Relative to the expected position on plan.*** If your project is due to be completed on 1 September, every day you are running late implies a day late at the end unless you can take action to recover this time. The simple question is: what is today's date and have you done as much as you expected, according to your plan? Similarly, if you only expected to have spent £100 and you have spent £200, then even though your overall budget is £10,000, you are going to be £100 over budget unless you can recoup this money.

- ***As a trend.*** Often forgotten but also important is the trend in progress, and projecting this trend into the future. For example, if you are three days behind after three weeks, it may not be a disaster if one identified task has overrun by three days. However, if the trend is that you are actually slipping one day every week and have underestimated everything by 20 per cent, then it indicates a major problem. A good project management saying is 'slippage occurs one day at a time'. You never find yourself suddenly two weeks late, you become late one day at a time. If you are two days into a 100-day project and you have only done the work your plan said you should have done in one day, you may not think you have a problem. You can almost certainly catch up one day when you need to. On the other hand, you are starting a bad trend as to date your project is taking twice as long as it should take. If this trend continues you are in trouble.

Sometimes you will find your project is moving ahead successfully. However, if everything always went according to plan, you probably would not need a project manager. The key reason for measuring progress is to understand when you must take action to speed things up.

If you are behind on time relative to the plan, or overspent, you do have the project's contingency to dip into. (In Chapter 3 I introduced adding contingency time and budget to a project, so you have some buffer in case things do not go according to plan.) Your aim should be to try to complete the project without using any contingency, but sometimes this cannot be done. Perhaps you have built 10 days' contingency into your plan, and find after a couple of weeks that you are running two days late, then you are still on target to complete your project within your contingency time. You should try to recover these two days by doing some other tasks more quickly, but this cannot always be done.

Do not forget the project's contingency is finite, and you may also need to use it later in the project. Hence another good rule of thumb is that you must use contingency no faster than the project's overall progress. For example, when you are halfway through, you should have used a maximum of half of your contingency, and preferably less. If after two weeks of a 12-week project you have used up the entire planned contingency, then you should be concerned and there is a high probability you are going to be late in finishing your project.

Issues

Problems that get in the way of project progress are called issues by project managers. Much of your time will be spent resolving issues. Issues can arise in any task you are doing whether or not it is a project and can take many forms. Your car may break down on the way to work: this is an issue. A colleague you needed to meet up with to complete some work may fall ill on the day you needed to meet her: this is an issue. A piece of equipment you wanted to buy for which you have £1,000 may cost £2,000 and you do not have the money: this is an issue. The software you are developing may be more complex than you thought and will take you 10 days to write rather than the five you planned: this is an issue. If these problems occurred as part of your project, you must find a way around them.

Project management is a structured way for ensuring an objective is met, and it has a structured process for resolving issues. By applying a structured process, issues are more likely to be resolved successfully. The steps to sort out issues are:

1. To make sure that the issue is identified and understood.

2. To develop some appropriate action to resolve the issue.

3. To allocate someone with responsibility for performing this action and hence resolving the issue.

4. To set a date for it to be resolved by.

5. To manage the task of resolving the issue by the set date.

Risks

You can prevent many of the worst issues by predicting what might go wrong in future, and taking some action now to avoid this prediction becoming true. This prediction is done by looking at project risks.

Because the future is not fully predictable, risks are present in everything that you do. You may be planning to launch a successful new product next year, but there is a risk your competitors may do something similar first. You may have some land on which you want to build a house, but there is a risk you will not get planning permission. You may want to fly to Indonesia next week, but there is a risk all the tickets have been sold already. You may be planning to paint your front room, but when you remove the existing wallpaper there is a risk that the plaster work underneath is in too bad a condition to be painted.

In a project, some of the risks will be related to the assumptions you made in planning the project. (These assumptions should have been documented in the Project Definition.) An assumption is, essentially, a best guess – not a fact. For every assumption there is a risk that it is not true, and if it is not true this will have an impact on your project. Consider two different examples in the Project Definitions in Chapter 2. Two assumptions were *'the wallpaper is OK to paint over'* and *'the market research we performed six months ago still provides a reliable view of the opportunities in the market'*. If either of these turns out not to be true then it will have a major impact on the projects. In the first case, when you start to paint it will not work, and your project will end up taking longer as you may have to find another way to paint the room. In the second case, if the market research is wrong then the product being developed may not sell and the whole project will be a failure.

If you know what the risks are, you can take action now to stop them occurring and having a negative impact on whatever you are trying to do. However, the list of possible risks is almost infinite, and so you need to find a way to focus on the most important risks only. To do this, you need to have some easy way of assessing and prioritising the risks you focus on. Prioritisation of risks can be done by looking at two aspects of risk: the *likelihood* that the risk will happen, and the *impact* on the project if it does.

There are many ways of measuring impact and likelihood. In practice, on all but the most complex of projects, it is sufficient to measure them by judgement and using a simple descriptive score. Both impact and likelihood can be judged to be high, medium or low. This descriptive score is going to be used for some simple arithmetic, so it is converted to a numeric score of 1 (low), 2 (medium) and 3 (high). The priority of your risk is simply the arithmetic result of multiplying the impact score by the likelihood score. The risks with the highest score are the ones you must worry about most, and have the highest priority to take some action about.

For example, consider the following four risks relevant to a project to launch a new product:

1. One of the tasks on your Project Plan is about to start. It is not on the critical path and does not need to be started for another three weeks. The person doing this task has had flu recently, but is now back in the office. You are concerned they may not be fully recovered and will take a further couple of days off. But you think the likelihood of this is low, and given the three weeks before the task needs to start, the impact will also be low if it does happen. Likelihood = 1, Impact = 1, so Priority = 1.

2. Your product will be packaged in a box. The box is essential to the sales. Your main supplier of boxes has financial troubles and it looks as if they will go bankrupt. However, you have two other suppliers who can easily and reliably provide the box. Therefore, likelihood of this risk occurring is high, but the impact is low. Likelihood = 3, Impact = 1, so Priority = 3.

3. You undertook some extensive market research before you started the project and this shows the product will be a success. Because you spent so much time and effort on the research, the likelihood of it being wrong is low – but the impact if it is wrong is very high. Likelihood = 1, Impact = 3, so Priority = 3.

4. Sixty per cent of the sales of this type of product happen at Christmas, so for the project to be a success it must be completed in time for a Christmas launch. You have planned your project and you can do it before Christmas, but there is no contingency in the plan and all the tasks have to be completed in the shortest time possible. There is a very high likelihood you will not meet the deadline and the impact is also very high. Likelihood = 3, Impact = 3, so Priority = 9.

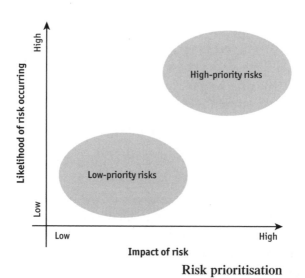

Risk prioritisation

If you were going to prioritise one of these risks to take some action about, it should be the fourth as it has both a high likelihood of happening and will have a high impact if it does. You can probably forget the first, and with the availability of alternative suppliers you have a good solution for the second. The third one needs to be explored a little more, for although the likelihood is low, the impact is so high that you may want to do even more research to make the likelihood of your research being wrong lower still.

Project management is a structured way for ensuring an objective is met – and it has a structured process for managing risks. By applying a structured process, risks are much less likely to occur and have a negative impact on the project. To manage risks:

1. Make sure that risks are identified and understood.

2. Focus on those risks that have the greatest combination of likelihood of occurring and possible impact on the project.

3. Develop a risk approach for each of the key risks.

4. Allocate someone with responsibility for carrying out this approach.

5. Set a date for this approach to be implemented.

6. Manage the task of getting the approach implemented, like any other task on the plan.

In terms of a strategy for handling any one risk, there are many different things you can do, but generically the approaches are to:

- *Ignore it altogether.* If the likelihood is low and the potential impact is also low, then it is perfectly valid to ignore the risk.

- *Monitor the risk.* Do nothing, but periodically review the risk to make sure it is not becoming more critical. Some risks have a good combination of low likelihood and low impact but need to be monitored as either of these can change in some situations. For instance, if your project required some work to be done outside, you may choose to do it in summer as the weather is driest. You could take some precaution against the rain. Alternatively, you can do nothing, but watch the weather forecast and only if it is deteriorating take precautions against the rain.

- *Reduce the likelihood of it occurring.* One way to reduce risk is to take action to reduce the likelihood of something occurring. For example, if you think you may not have enough money in a bank account to pay your bills, if you put more in the bank, the likelihood of running out is reduced. You have not reduced the impact if you do run out of money but you have reduced the likelihood of running out.

- *To reduce the impact if it does occur.* The alternative way to reduce risk is to take actions now to reduce the impact of a risk upon you if it does occur. For example, consider again the situation where you think you may not have enough money in a bank account. If a friend agrees to pay your bills, when you run out you have reduced the impact of this risk. You have not changed the likelihood of running out of money but you have reduced the impact.

- *To have some contingency plan in place.* This is similar to the previous approach, except instead of taking action now, you develop a plan to implement only if the risk happens.

Changes

How often have you had a clear idea in your mind of what you want, but when you started to do some further work found that your ideas change? Projects are not immune to such changes, and project customers will often ask for some change to the deliverables while a project is already under way and fully planned.

The problem is that you have agreed a time and cost within which to complete the project. If you change the deliverables, you may also impact the end date, or the cost of the project. Given that project management is a structured way for ensuring an objective is met, it has a structured process for managing change. By applying a structured process, changes will only be undertaken if they are agreed with the customer, and he or she understands the impact of them on the project. The approach to manage change is to:

1. Ensure change is controlled, and no change is made without using the change control process.

2. Assess every change in terms of its impact on the project. For example, does it increase time, budget required, or the level of risk?

STEP 4: MANAGE DELIVERY

3. Accept the change only if the project customer agrees to the change, having first understood the impact on the project of the change.

Poor change control is a very common reason for project failure.

The step-by-step guide
STEP 4 – Managing delivery

Step 4.1 Start the project

Projects do not start by themselves just because you want them to, or because you have developed a plan. Projects require a push to get started. This push is something you, as the project manager, must give the project team.

Before you give your project this push, it is usually worth having a final conversation with your project customer, to:

- Confirm the Project Definition and that there are no last-minute changes.

- Clarify the implications of the Project Plan. Make sure the customer understands and accepts what the project will cost and how long it will take (including contingency).

- Confirm that you have access to the resources you need and it is OK for you now to start using them.

Once this is done it is time to get the project started. The push you give a project is to communicate with everyone involved in the project. Each person in the project team needs to know:

- What their role on the project is, and what tasks you are expecting them to do in what order.

- When they need to do these tasks.

- What resources they will have access to in order to complete their work.

- How you expect them to keep you updated on progress.

At this stage it is also worth asking all members of the project team for any issues, concerns, ideas and suggestions. (It is not too late to change the plan if someone has an idea of how to do it better.) It is also important to try and motivate and excite people about the project, as well-motivated people are much more likely to work hard and deliver the result you want.

For a small project this can be done by talking individually to each project team member. For a large project it is useful to run a meeting called a mobilisation session. This is a meeting in which you bring the whole team together and explain the Project Definition, the Project Plan, make sure everyone knows their roles, and respond to any questions people have.

Now the project is rolling!

Step 4.2 Plan your day

You have a complete Project Definition, a good Project Plan and a Project Budget. You have briefed the project team and they are now working. So what do you do on a day-to-day basis? The funny thing is that you are about to manage a piece of work which is planned out step by step in your Project Plan, but the one thing that is not planned in the same way is your job as the project manager. Do not be under any misapprehension though, there is plenty to do!

Your job is to make sure that everything that needs to happen, to keep the project going towards the desired end result, happens. Anything can occur on a project and you should start every day by thinking:

- What things are causing most difficulty to the project now (typically related to progress and issues)?

- What are the things that are most likely to cause problems to the project in future (normally relating to risks and changes)?

- What actions are my responsibility to undertake?

- Which are the most important things that I need to resolve now?

Having thought this through, you know what you need to overcome so you can plan out what you are going to do today. This will need to be prioritised and changed on an ongoing basis as different issues occur. They will occur every day.

For a project manager it is important to understand that you are not personally responsible for doing everything (unless it is a one-person project) – there is a project team. But you are responsible for ensuring that everything happens, and that someone in this team does every-thing that needs to be done. Your role is like the conductor of an orchestra: you play no instrument, but unless you do your work, the sound from the orchestra will be a cacophony and not the wonderful concert desired.

You know your objective. It is clear. You know how you will get there. This is also clear. On top of this, you have a set of tools and techniques to allow you to manage the project. The remainder of this chapter gives you the tools to do what the project manager needs to do:

- Steps 4.3 to 4.7 are ways to give yourself the information to make decisions about what you need to focus on.

- Steps 4.8 to 4.10 are how you go about doing things once you know what they are.

Step 4.3 Collect information and reports

As your project progresses you need to collect information to determine what you should be doing as the project manager. If you are working on a project, by yourself and for yourself, then this will happen automati-cally as the project goes along. However, when there are many people working on a project, you need to put effort into collecting information from them as the work progresses.

Some information will come to you naturally on a day-to-day basis as you interact with people and ask them to do things. However, it is good practice to have a formal update meeting once a week with the members of your project team. You should try to make this meeting as short as possible so it does not get in the way of working on the project. The information you want from each team member is:

- What they did in the last week. Was it as planned, and what was produced?

- What they plan to do in the next week. Does that match the project plan?

- Are there any new issues, risks or changes they need to raise?

- What is the progress on any issues, risks or changes they are working on?

Following this meeting you are in a position to report to your customer. You need to consolidate the information from all the people in the project and only provide the key information to the customer, consisting of:

- Overall project status. Are you on track or not?

- If not, what will you do to bring the project back on track?

- Your current view of the likely outcome of the project.

- An overview of what was done last week and what will be done next week.

- Any decisions you need from the customer, for example approvals to changes.

A simple progress report should be produced which is at most one page of A4. A suitable example of a report format is shown in Table 4.1. Although this report is very short and simple, it provides most customers with all the information they need to have a sufficient understanding of the project status. The aim is not to overload your customer with detailed information, but to provide enough to give a good idea of status, to avoid them getting any surprises if there are problems with the project, and to give them confidence that the project is in safe hands!

PROJECT REPORT	Project name:	Office re-fit project	
	Reporting period:	Week commencing 18 July	
Project on track?	No – 2 weeks late currently	Estimated completion date	5 Sep
		Estimated completion budget	£237,430
Description of status	– The project is running well with few critical issues or problems. However, the initial delay in finding a suitable contractor has not been recovered and we continue to run 2 weeks late. In addition, the contractor has advised us that our initial estimates for time to fit the offices were overly optimistic and so we now estimate a completion date of 2 September. This is within our overall contingency, but does give concern that if any unforeseen problems arise we may be late. – One improvement against plan, the contractor's work is slightly cheaper than expected. – If the proposed change to expand the project to 110 staff rather than the current 100 is approved, the project will be extended by a further 4 days and £8,800.		
Main actions done this week	– Removal of old furniture. – Fitted carpets.		
Main actions to be completed next week	– Start installation of new furniture.		
Issues to be aware of	– Desks cost has risen to £325 per desk, meaning an increase in costs of £2,500.		
Risks to be aware of	– Risk of late delivery of complete set of furniture. – Risk of late delivery of final batch of 25 sets of desktop equipment. 75 received and ready to install, but 25 missing. However, this will not immediately impact critical path.		
Approvals required	– Change raised to expand project to 110 desks.		

Table 4.1 **Example of a project report**

Step 4.4 Monitor and manage progress

The project manager should be monitoring the progress of the project continuously. This will happen informally all the time as you work on the project, and once a week formally with the project team in your review meeting. The basic process for monitoring and managing progress is to look at what tasks are completed and what should have been completed, and then ask yourself the following series of questions:

- Are you on schedule or not, relative to the plan? Are there any trends you are worried about?

- If there is any slippage, what is the impact? Are the late tasks on the critical path or not?

- How much time are you late? So how much do you need to recover to bring yourself back on track? Are you likely to slip beyond your contingency time?

- What options are there for recovering this time?

- Which option is best?

Key drivers for success **5** Drive progress every day

A project has a defined objective which is meant to be complete within a predefined amount of time. On some days you will find the project team are successful in moving the project forward, on other days they will be less so. Perhaps the task they are doing is complex, or a difficult issue has arisen, or simply the team is not motivated on that day. No one works flat-out all the time, but in your role as the project manager you need to ensure that progress is being made all the time.

When you relax and do not push the project team to keep delivering, they will also tend to relax and progress will slow down. Usually if the odd day or two is lost it can be recovered, but if you are not careful you will start a trend for the project to be late.

When slippage has occurred, there are an infinite variety of actions you can take. The actions you choose will depend on the specific situation you are in, but typically include:

- *Getting your team to do subsequent tasks more quickly.* This is often the simplest way of recovering time. It is not always possible, but often if you ask people to focus on your project and put in a little more effort, some slippage can be recovered. If you work to keep the project team motivated and interested in the project, they will often automatically make up for any slippage that occurs. This only really works if you are tracking your project closely and you need the team to catch up a small amount of time, such as a few days.

- *Accepting the slippage and using some contingency.* This is a valid option, but even if you are going to use up some of your contingency you should see if there is another way of recovering the time.

- *Adding more resources.* This sometimes works, but it means you may convert a slippage in time into extra budget.

- *Looking at alternative ways to do what you are trying to do.* There are lots of ways projects can be done differently. Looking at the tasks, are there any that can be shortened? Or can any dependencies be removed so tasks can be done sooner?

- *Changing the project in some way.* If you reduce your scope and deliver less, the project can sometimes be done more quickly. This should not be done lightly and always requires your customer's approval, but if you really are going to be late you should ask your customer: 'Would you prefer the project to be late, or on time but deliver less?'

- *Doing nothing.* Accept the slippage and be late. This is a possible option and sometimes you have no choice, but it is not always acceptable to your project customer. If you keep doing this you should ask yourself what value you are actually adding as the project manager.

Although the progress of a project follows a well-defined plan, the reality is that day-to-day working is very dynamic and constantly raising challenges. You must respond flexibly to the challenges that arise, and recognise if what you are doing is not working, as there is certainly another approach that will work better. When problems arise that seem intractable, try to think in different ways and usually you will find a way round them. Also, don't forget to use the project team – when there is a problem, asking everyone in the team for solutions will often throw up innovative and practical solutions.

The best project managers adopt the attitude that all problems can be solved, and that by thinking and rapidly applying the thinking, all projects can be successful. This is not to say they do impossible things, but by being flexible and creative in overcoming obstacles on projects, they get around most problems.

A good project manager faces challenges such as late tasks with the attitude that there is always a solution, and actively seeks to find and implement it.

Step 4.5 Identify and resolve issues

At the start of a project you should have very few issues. If there are any, they should have been documented as problems in your Project Definition. However, issues will arise as the project progresses. Unforeseen problems have a habit of occurring; in fact one of the most important tasks of a project manager is in ensuring such problems are resolved. Success in a project is not about having no problems, it is about delivering in spite of them! What differentiates really good project managers from average ones is the ability to overcome problems rather than accepting them as facts of life.

As issues are identified they should be reported to you. This should be done by all members of the project team as soon as they are identified. To be sure you are aware of all problems, ask all team members at the weekly review session if there are any new issues. You must keep on top of issues, as the number of them can build up. A large project may have tens or even hundreds of issues.

Once you become aware of issues, document them in an issues log, which provides a simple tool to allow you to manage them. For every issue identify:

- What the issue is.

- When it was identified.

- What impact it is having on the project.

- Who is going to resolve the issue? This person is usually called the issue owner.

- What the action to resolve the issue is.

- When it needs to be resolved by.

- When the next update on progress to fix the issue is due.

- Whether it is open (still a problem to the project) or closed (it has been resolved and is no longer a problem). This is shown on the issues log as 'O' for open, and 'C' for closed.

An example of part of an issues log for the office re-fit project is shown in Table 4.2.

PROJECT ISSUE LOG

No.	Issue description	When identified	Impact on project	Owner	Action to resolve	Date to be resolved	Update due	O/C
			Project name: Office re-fit project					
			Last updated: 8 July					
1	We do not have agreement about the security around the wireless LAN.	01 July	Unless this is agreed we cannot allow staff to connect to network.	Adam	Arrange session with interested parties and decide on security.	8 July	N/A	C
2	There are only two sets of keys for the office – and as they are security keys we cannot easily get more cut.	31 May	Without easy access to the office for all staff involved in the project, as and when they require, we risk slowing down progress.	Dave	Allocate one member of the project team to be on site during all office hours. Immediately start process of getting additional keys cut and allocate to nominated team members.	14 June	Confirm who is going to be on-site all the time.	C
3	Dave's wife has been taken ill and he needs to take some time off to look after his children.	10 June	We cannot progress on task 4 on the project without Dave's skills, and this will delay completion.	Project Manager	Source contract staff to support task while Dave is off.	4 July	27 June Met temps and candidate selected.	C

4	The lift has broken down and we cannot get furniture to 3rd floor offices.	16 June	We cannot progress with task 3 on the plan and without this being completed we will delay the project.	Project Manager	Chase lift maintenance crew. Offer extra payment if they come in overnight to fix. In interim contract 3–4 removal staff to carry desks upstairs.	20 June	19 June Confirm repair complete.	C
5	The desks cost more than expected.	21 June	The desks are £325 each rather than £300, resulting in a £2,500 overspend. We have sufficient contingency budget to cover this – so if it cannot be resolved we will accept higher cost.	Dave	Try to: – Negotiate discount with supplier. – Seek alternative supplier (though not expected to be successful at this time). However if not possible, order desks at higher price as this is on the critical path.	27 June	Desks ordered at higher cost.	C
6	The carpet has been delivered but we are 150m² short.	5 July	We cannot complete upstairs offices without this.	Dave	Carpet the area we can and start to install in those areas. Chase supplier for additional carpet and hold back all payment until it arrives.	21 July	14 July Dave to report to project manager on progress.	O

No.	Issue description	When identified	Impact on project	Owner	Action to resolve	Date to be resolved	Update due	O/C
7	There is an area in the office which may be unable to receive wireless signal.	6 July	We will not be able to offer wireless access to all staff.	Dave	Get quote from contractor to put additional cabling for another router in place.	1 August (or will delay installation).	13 July Return quote from contractor.	O
8	The desktop equipment supplier can only provide 75 sets in the first batch.	8 July	We need 100 sets for all the staff, and so 25 staff will be without desktop equipment.	Mike	Take the first batch of 75. The remaining 25 are not required until late August – get commitment to this from supplier. If necessary we can go live without them, but this is not ideal.	29 July	22 July Update on status of order.	O

Table 4.2 Example of an issues log

You should manage the actions in the issues log like any other task on the project and ensure they are being progressed. It is best to review this log on a daily basis to make sure issues are being resolved. Regularly contact owners of issues and ask them to confirm progress is being made. If an issue is having a major impact on the project, or actions are due for completion in the next day or two, phone whoever is responsible for the action daily and make sure it is done.

At your weekly review meeting check that the owners are undertaking their actions. Important information in this table is the 'Date to be resolved', which needs to be treated as if it is a task end date on the plan and should not slip. Additionally, because some issues do take several weeks to resolve, by putting information in the 'Update due' column, you can start to ensure that progress is being made even if the issue is not fully resolved.

A sign of a project in trouble is when issues do not get resolved and the list keeps on getting longer and longer.

Remember your job is to manage the project, not to do everything. Although you can own some issues, you should not be the owner of all of them unless it is a one-man project team.

Step 4.6 Identify and manage risks

At the beginning of a project, think of all the risks that exist and prioritise them by the impact and likelihood, as described in the section 'Risks' at the start of this chapter. Start by reviewing the assumptions in your Project Definition and decide if any of these add significant risk to your project.

For larger projects, a good way to do this is to run a brainstorm with the project team as part of the mobilisation session. Once you have this initial log, you need to keep it updated. If additional risks are identified, they should be reported to you. At your weekly review session ask all team members if there are any new risks.

Once you become aware of risks, then you should document them in a risk log. For every risk identify:

● What the risk is.

● What the likelihood of it occurring is.

- What the impact will be, if it occurs.

- What its overall priority is.

- Who is responsible for managing the risk.

- What the next action to resolve this risk is.

- When any actions need to be completed.

- What the current status of the risk is.

An example of a risk log is given in Table 4.3.

PROJECT RISK LOG				Project name:	Office re-fit project		
				Last updated:	18 July		
No.	Risk	Likelihood	Impact	Priority	Owner	Proposed action	Date to be actioned	Current status
1	This is an unfamiliar project to plan and experience is limited and therefore there is a risk of underestimating time and budget.	M (2)	M (2)	4	Project Manager	We have put some contingency into the plan to reduce the likelihood of this risk.	No action – manage as part of project.	As part of normal progress updates.
2	The project extends beyond the time at which the existing offices have to be evacuated, and the new office is not ready for staff. The current date we must leave the existing office is 1 October.	L (1)	H (3)	3	Project Manager	With sufficient contingency this has a low likelihood. However we must keep monitoring the situation. With two months' notice the landlord will extend existing offices – at a premium price for an additional one month. We must decide by 1 August whether this is necessary.	Decision meeting scheduled for 22 July	Open and still a risk. Try to resolve this week and decide whether to have extension or not.

▶

No.	Risk	Likelihood	Impact	Priority	Owner	Proposed action	Date to be actioned	Current status
3	The office we are taking over is in an old building and has been vacant for some time. We have assumed there are no significant problems which will need to be resolved.	M (2)	H (3)	6	Dave	Perform full survey of office before finalising plan and committing to timescales.	3 June	Closed.
4	In our original plan we have assumed we only needed wireless routers at four points in the office. It now looks as if we may need a fifth.	M	H	6	Adam	Survey the office and check if an additional router is required. If so build into the plans to source and install.	Must be resolved by 29 July.	Open – testing due this week. Change request prepared in case required.
5	We need to switch off the electricity for a few hours, which requires agreement of all other tenants in building. This may be difficult to get.	L	M	2	Contractor	Monitor situation.		Open

6	Concern that the new desk furniture will not be liked by the staff, creating a bad feeling about the move of offices.	L	L	1	Dave	No action required.	Closed
7	The new desks bought are not suitable for the new building.	L	H	3	Dave	Test desk brought into the office and fitted.	Closed
8	The existing cupboard space within the office is insufficient for our needs. We do not intend to install any new cupboards.	L	L	1	Dave	No action – current understanding is that it is enough. If a problem there is space for additional cupboards.	Monitor
9	We do not have the landlord's permission for the work we intend to carry out.	L	H	3	Project Manager	Resolve via facilities – ensure we have evidence of full approval.	Closed

Table 4.3 Example of a risks log

You should manage the actions in the risk log like any other task on the project and ensure they are being completed. At your weekly review meeting check that this is happening.

Step 4.7 Manage changes

As the project progresses, it is common for the understanding of the end goal to improve, and as a result for it to become apparent that something on the project needs to change. Alternatively, the customer may decide that the end deliverables are not now what is needed and he or she desires to change them. Unless changes are controlled, you will not know what the outcome of the project will be. The project may be late or it could fail. If change is continuous, the project may simply never finish. The way to control changes is via a change management process.

The change management process uses a change control form. Once changes have been identified they should be documented with the following information:

- Document what the change is.

- Describe why the change is being proposed.

- Identify when the change needs to be accepted by, if it is to work.

- Identify the impact of the change. Will it change the length of the project, or the cost? Does it change the level of quality or risk?

- Note what the proposed action with regard to this change is.

- Keep track of the current status of the change: it can either be 'in review'; it can be 'accepted' (i.e. it is agreed and has been built into plans); or 'rejected' (i.e. the project will continue unchanged).

- Sign off from the customer to the change.

An example of a completed change form is given in Table 4.4.

PROJECT CHANGE	Project name: office re-fit project
	Last updated: 16 July

Description of proposed change

The current project will deliver desks and equipment for 100 staff. This change would increase, by an additional 10 desks, to 110.

Reason for change

This would provide the opportunity to shut down the small office in London Road, which has 10 staff in it. Originally this was not viable as the lease is for a further two years. However, the landlord has agreed he will allow us to move out early without penalty so he can redevelop the site. There is floor-space in the new office and if done, we will save the rental on the London Road office from 1 November.

When this needs to be agreed by	22 July

Impact on the project

Timescale: +4 days
Cost: £7,000 for furniture and desktop equipment, £1,800 for additional labour.
Other: Some minor risk implications. We already have a problem sourcing 100 sets of desktop equipment. This will exacerbate that issue. We can go live without this with staff working directly from laptops for a while. However, the furniture was ordered about two weeks ago and will arrive in two weeks. The supplier has indicated he can provide the additional 10 within a couple of days of completing the main order, as long as he receives the order by 25 July.

▶

Proposed action			
We propose that this change is accepted. The timescale impact is minimal, and cost is modest compared to savings.			
Status	In review	Rejected	Accepted
	✓		
Customer approval	not yet approved – for review this week		
Date of customer approval	not yet approved – for review this week		

Table 4.4 **Example of a change form**

As part of your weekly review with your customer, you should go through the proposed changes and how they will impact the project. Your customer should then decide whether to accept or reject them. If the change is accepted, it needs to be explained to other project team members and, where necessary, the Project Plan and Project Budget must be updated.

For big projects, or those which have a lot of changes, you may need to keep track of all the changes in a change log. An example of a change log is given in Table 4.5.

PROJECT CHANGE LOG		Project name:	Office re-fit project	
		Last updated:	25 July	
No.	Change description	Owner	Current status	Update due
1	Include refitting of all cupboard space in office.	Dave	Rejected	n/a
2	Change screen to 40" for 6 graphic designers' desks.	Mary	Accepted	n/a
3	Expansion to 110 desks.	Dave	In review	29/07
4	Expansion of project to include upgrading wireless LAN.	Adam	In review	29/07

Table 4.5 Example of a change log

Step 4.8 Take action to ensure the project's success

By performing the previous parts of Step 4 you understand your project's progress, you understand issues and risks and the changes that are being asked for. You have all the information you need to manage the project, but managing a project is not simply about understanding it, it is about *taking action*.

Key drivers for success	7	Be the project manager!

There are always lots of things to do on a project: tasks that need to be completed, issues that need to be resolved, risks and changes that need to be analysed, and customers who need to be briefed on progress. There is sometimes a temptation for the project manager to get involved in doing the work and not focus on managing it.

▶

The title 'project manager' is a deliberate one. It is not 'project doer', 'project team member', or 'project worker'. The role is to manage the project. It is an essential role. If people simply work on a project without someone looking over, coordinating, directing and controlling all the different activities, it is unlikely to be a success unless it is a very simple task.

Of course you may be working on a project by yourself. This usually happens on very small projects. On very small projects you usually won't have a full-time project manager. You will get involved in doing the tasks on the plan as well. However, even in this situation, do not confuse the work of doing tasks with managing the project. And if a customer tries to encourage you to be both the project manager and one of the project team on a project of any size or complexity, say no. It won't work!

A good analogy is with the conductor of an orchestra. No one expects a great conductor to pick up an instrument halfway through a concert and start playing. Everyone understands that his or her role is to conduct, and that this is a crucial role. The same should be true for a project manager, your role is to manage the project, and this is an essential role.

Action can take many forms: you may need to ask permission to access a building; you may need to call someone to check they are doing the work they are meant to be doing; you may need to buy some stationery for the project team; you may need to hire a contractor to get some work done more quickly; you may need to talk to a project team member to motivate them to work faster, and so on. The actions will cover the spectrum from large and complex tasks through to simple, quick acts. Whatever the actions are, they do not just need to be decided upon and planned, you need to make sure they happen!

Some project managers have the false impression that project management is just concerned with monitoring and reporting, with some supporting administration. These are important parts of project management, but the key role of the project manager is to keep progress going on the project and to take whatever actions are necessary to keep this happening.

The action you take depends on what the information you have col-lected shows. You must assess it all and decide what needs to be done and implement the action in the most appropriate manner. Project man-agement processes and tools show when you need to take action (for example, to recover time so you are not late or to overcome issues) but they cannot tell you how to do this. Now is the time to use your common sense and experience to come up with solutions – and having deter-mined solutions, to implement them.

Table 4.6 shows some examples of typical problems on projects and what actions can be taken to overcome them.

Typical problems	Constructive actions
When the project team starts to create a deliverable, they find the definition provided by the customer is not clear enough.	• Get the project team to succinctly define the area(s) of ambiguity. • Arrange a short workshop with the customer to clarify all ambiguous definitions.

When the project team starts to create a deliverable, they find that it cannot easily be created in the way it is defined without significant delay or cost.	• Generate three versions of the Project Plan, Budget and Definition:
	  1. A revised plan and budget for the deliverable as described.
	  2. A revised definition to meet the original cost and time.
	  3. A recommended balance between the two.
	• Present the options to the customer and agree which to follow.

A member of the project team is unavailable due to illness and it is unclear how long the individual will be unavailable for.	• Assume the illness will last, i.e. do not be over-optimistic on speed of recovery.
	• Assess the impact on the project of not having this person.
	• If impact is significant then look for alternative ways of getting the work done:
	  1. Can you get another person easily?
	  2. Is it possible for other team members to do the work, possibly paying for overtime?
	  3. Can you find and use a contractor?
	  4. Is it possible to buy a service in from an external company?
	• Select best option and implement.

The project is running late.	• Determine if the delay in progress is important or not (some lateness may not be a problem, it depends on the individual situation). • Review the plan and determine if the time can be recovered as the project progresses, or by using contingency. • Identify other options to recover time. • Assess if any option is viable and which is best. • Implement chosen option.

Table 4.6 **Examples of project actions to overcome common problems**

Step 4.9 Keep your customer informed

The nature of projects is such that sometimes there will be problems. An unforeseen issue will arise which jeopardises the project, or a risk happens that you cannot do anything about. As the project manager, your job is to try and stop this happening, but if it does happen, to minimise the impact on the project. However well you apply structure, rigour and good discipline, you are not a miracle worker and sometimes the project will be late or overspent.

One of the key differences between a good project manager and a poor one is that a good project manager makes sure that a project delivers no surprises. If the project goes wrong, there should at least have been a prediction that it might go wrong (this is the purpose of the risk log). And when it goes wrong, your customer should know; it should not be a secret. Although giving bad news about a project is never a pleasant thing to do, hiding it and leaving your customer with a potentially bigger problem is far worse.

Often customers are very happy with projects that are late compared to the original plan, or a little overspent. However, this is only true when they have been kept informed, and understand why it is late and more expensive. Through good information flows, as the project progresses, the customer should be briefed if the project is expected to be late.

Key drivers for success	8	Communicate continuously

Project management is, at its heart, people management. Your role is to complete the project with the people you have available to work in the team. It requires listening to and understanding what your customer wants, explaining what you want people to do, instructing the team on the order of tasks, watching for problems as they arise, and keeping everyone aware of progress.

Although project management sometimes requires you to sit by yourself, to think through what needs to be done and the best way to do it, it is work that relies on the regular and ongoing interaction with people. The best project managers spend ▶

a large proportion of their time communicating with customers, the project team, and anyone who can impact progress on the project. This ongoing action of listening and talking is key to successful project management.

If you are not spending a high proportion of your time listening, talking, asking and answering questions, then you are probably not managing the project.

Step 4.10 Update the Project Plan or Project Budget

The Project Plan and the Project Budget are your predictions at the start of the project of what it will take to deliver the project. As such, your success is about meeting the timescale and the budget agreed. However, the plan and budget are also tools to help you manage the project as it happens. In some situations the plan or the budget become so different from reality that you need to update them. This should be an uncommon occurrence as what you are effectively doing is changing the way you will deliver the project. You are also changing the basis of measurement of the project.

If any change you make moves a milestone on the plan, alters the overall timescale or changes the budget for a project, you must agree it with the project customer.

The times to make changes are:

- If you realise that there is a better way to complete the project. This does sometimes happen and is obviously a good thing!

- When you implement agreed changes. If a customer agrees to a change that results in the timeline or budget for the project changing, then the plan or budget must be updated to reflect this.

- When the issue(s) becomes unresolvable in the timescale or budget originally allocated and there is a significant resulting overrun in time or money. Changing the plan or budget is not something to be done lightly, and should be done with a heavy heart, but occasionally it is necessary.

When the plan or budget does need to be updated, then go through the relevant parts of Chapter 2 again.

Key tips

- Remember, slippage occurs one day at a time. Keep on top of progress. You do not suddenly become two weeks late, you become two weeks late *one day at a time.*

- To understand your progress, you should look at your absolute position relative to the plan, and the trend in progress.

- Contingency should not be used up faster than a project is progressing.

- After identification, risks and issues should have actions allocated to a project team member to resolve them. This action should be managed like any other task on a project with a target date for completion.

- Do not let change happen to a project in an uncontrolled manner.

- Project management is about taking action to overcome anything that gets in the way of meeting your objectives.

- Good project managers ensure their customers know how the project is progressing on a regular basis.

- The likelihood of success in projects will be increased not only by following the correct process, and understanding what a project manager needs to do, but by applying this knowledge in the most constructive way. Be hands-on, communicate regularly and manage your customer's expectations.

TO DO NOW

- Get ready to start your project. Are you comfortable to run a mobilisation session for the project team? It's worth planning this out fully. Do it well and you will have a motivated and energised project team; do it badly and confidence in your skills as the project manager may be dented.

- Get your project administration clear. Make sure you have all the templates and forms you need, know how to use them, and are clear about who on the project team has access to them. Will you send forms out by email, make them available on a shared drive, or use hard copy paper versions only?

- Plan out your personal schedule and how you will manage actions, issues, risks, changes and progress.

- Make sure the project team members have the meetings you want them to attend in their diaries.

- Make sure your customer is available regularly to discuss issues and progress. Forward book an hour a week in their diary. Even if you don't know precisely what you will use it for, you will find you have plenty to discuss every week.

Taking it further: Risk and stakeholder management

One of the most important concepts in project management, and the area those new to project management often find hardest to understand the criticality of, is risk.

Projects are associated with risk for a wide variety of reasons. A useful term that helps to understand risk is *VUCA*, which stands for volatile, uncertain, complex and ambiguous. Essentially, VUCA says we work in a world we cannot fully predict. Projects work in an environment which is VUCA. This means with even the most detailed analysis and best planning techniques there are risks that may impact project timescales, costs, quality and overall viability.

Project management has a specific set of approaches to managing risk, which come under the title *risk management*. In this chapter, I introduced a simple and robust form of project management which will work in many project situations. However, there are more powerful forms of risk management for use in especially complex or risky projects.

More advanced project risk management introduces the concepts of *opportunities*. An opportunity is a positive risk which offers a chance that the project could go better than intended. By using risk management to identify opportunities as well as risks, project managers can find ways of improving a project's performance.

In some projects risk management is not just an important supporting process, but can become the core process of the project, where the whole project is shaped around understanding and overcoming risks.

Some project methods, such as Agile (introduced in the section 'Taking it further' at the end of Step 1), are based on the view that short projects are less prone to risk, and that by using an iterative approach the project can adapt and change as the customer and project team's understanding of the project evolve.

To the inexperienced project management can seem a rather dry topic that is best done by an individual working at a desk thinking about plans and producing various reports and charts. These are important parts of project management, but as its heart project management is concerned with interacting and dealing with people. Rather than being a dry skill for the individual, it is a dynamic capability centred on people and people management skills.

One group of people the project manager must deal with are the project team. Through this book we have talked about the team. The other group of people the project manager must deal with are all the people external to the project who have an interest in it – that is the project's stakeholders.

Most projects have an assortment of stakeholders. What experienced project managers soon learn is that it is how well you deal with stakeholders, set and manage their expectations, and keep them positively engaged in a project that is one of the most important factors in project management. Sometimes it is the most important. I have seen project managers succeed despite failing to deliver their plans because they manage to keep their stakeholders happy. I have never seen project managers succeed if they irritate or upset their stakeholders, irrespective of the actual success of the underlying project.

This is part of a wider truth, that while project management is full of special technical 'hard' skills, it is usually 'soft' skills such as communications, expectation management, dealing with people, negotiating, influencing and so forth which are most critical to a project manager's success. This is often forgotten. If you want to run simple projects for yourself, you can get away with forgetting this. If you want to run complex projects involving lots of people, you cannot.

One specific aspect of project management concerned with handling people is stakeholder management. It is worth developing a practical understanding of stakeholder management as well as the other soft skills required by project management. Stakeholder management is conceptually easy, but requires practice to master.

FURTHER READING

- **Simple risk management:** Newton, R., *Brilliant Checklists for Project Managers*, 2nd Edition, Pearson Education, 2014

- **Project risk management:** Chapman, C. and Ward, S., *Project Risk Management: Processes, Techniques and Insights*, 2nd Edition, John Wiley, 2003

- **Stakeholder management:** Eskerod, P. and Lund Jepsen, A., *Project Stakeholder Management*, Gower, 2013

- **Human side to project management:** Newton, R., *The Project Manager: Mastering the Art of Delivery*, 2nd Edition, FT Prentice Hall, 2009

Step 5

Complete your project

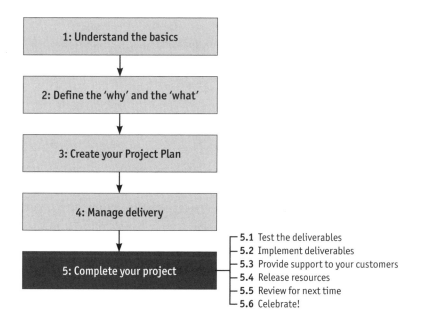

1: Understand the basics

2: Define the 'why' and the 'what'

3: Create your Project Plan

4: Manage delivery

5: Complete your project

THIS CHAPTER COVERS:

- How to finish a project – which encompasses ensuring the deliverables are complete, correct and usable by your customer.

The activities described in this chapter are performed at the end of a project. However, the tasks described take time and use up resources, so they need to be included in the Project Plan. That's why in Chapter 3 I suggested reviewing the contents of this chapter to ensure the tasks are planned in advance. The tasks in this chapter are often essential to a successful project, but often are forgotten at the outset. You can avoid this mistake, and always build them into project plans and budgets.

THE CENTRAL POINT IS:

- Successful projects end in a controlled way, with the project manager making sure all the loose ends are tied up. This often requires testing the deliverables, and making sure your customer understands how to use them.

Setting the scene

Suppose you have been running a project to write a bespoke app for a business that will be used by all the business's employees on their smart-phones or tablets. The project team of five people has worked on this for six weeks and has just completed writing the app. Is your project over?

No. There are still some things to do. First, just because you have coded the app, it does not mean it works properly – the software has to be tested. Once it is tested you may have greater confidence that it works, but will your customer be able to use it? Normally you have to spend some time encouraging their employees to install it. For specialist or complex apps you may need to show them how to use it, and possibly running some structured training. Having done this, a few days later some employees may have additional questions or they may identify a bug that your testing did not pick up. This is why it is good practice to provide some support to your customer for a limited period after the deliverables have been handed over, to answer their questions and fix any faults they find.

Now you can start to close your project down. The project team can be 'released', that is let go to work on another project to develop some other app. But you probably don't want them all to go at once. They should be let go at different times, as the relevant parts of the project complete. Also, any money you have not spent from your Project Budget needs to be given back to your customer.

If you are never going to run a project again perhaps you can stop now. However, if you think you might run projects in future, it is worth reviewing this project. What did you do well, and what could have been done better? If you know what to do better and what was done well, when you start to develop your next app you should do it even more successfully.

If the project was a success and your customer was happy with the app you developed, it may be worth having a small celebration. You deserve it, after all you have completed a project!

Introduction to completing your project

If you have followed Steps 1 to 4 in this book, you should now have a successfully running project. However, one of the things that really differentiates the average project manager from the outstanding one is the way the project ends. Success in projects is not just about producing deliverables, it is about producing deliverables and giving them over to your customer in the best way possible and making sure they can be used to meet the 'why' defined in your Project Definition.

The way you need to complete your project varies considerably, depending on the nature of the project and the deliverables. There are many factors to consider when ending a project, most of which you will be aware of simply through common sense. However, there are some critical steps for some projects, which are regularly forgotten:

1. *Test the deliverables.* Do they work, and do they work as expected? This does not apply to all deliverables. But deliverables like apps, software, new machines and so on should be tested to ensure they work properly.

2. *Help the customer to use the deliverables.* Some deliverables need to be explained to people, or implemented for them. On some occasions people need to be trained in how to use the deliverable. Again, this does not apply to all deliverables. For example, if your deliverable is a report, then customers usually don't need to be shown how to use it. However, some deliverables are not so obvious to use – if you have a new computer system, people need to be trained in it. A new office layout may need to be explained to the staff moving into it. New ways of working, such as revised processes and procedures, may require you not only to train people in how to use them, but also to convince them that the new processes are an improvement. If your deliverable is a new business policy you will need to educate staff on the new policy, and you may also need to explain the implications of the policy and how they impact all aspects of their work. A new machine in a factory will require the operators to be trained. Whatever your deliverables, you must consider what help the final users and customers may need to gain the full benefit from it.

3. *Support the customer while they get used to the deliverables, and for a short period when they find out if they are working properly.* Some deliverables require support even if a customer has been trained how to use them. This may be because they are particularly complicated or because some problems do not immediately show up. So, for example, with new software, it is usual for customers to find bugs after it has been implemented which the developers have to fix. Similarly, if some building work is done for a customer, it is common for them to pull together 'snagging' lists of all the small things that are not quite right with the building.

The nature of the tasks you need to carry out in Step 5 of the project will vary, depending on the type of project and the nature of the deliverables. Hence this section is less a list of specific instructions and more a set of questions to ask yourself. By asking the questions in this chapter you should be able to derive the tasks you need to do relevant to the specific situation.

The step-by-step guide
STEP 5 – Completing your project

Step 5.1 Test the deliverables

If you are responsible for a project, it is right for your customer to expect you to manage it to produce deliverables that work, and which meet all the requirements agreed. To do this you may need to test the deliverables. There are many ways to do this, and the testing required depends entirely on the type of deliverable. How you test a new car is completely different from how you test software, or from how you would test a new building you had just built. However, each deliverable should be tested before you are completely confident they meet your expectations.

While the actual tests vary between deliverables, there are some generic questions you need to ask to test any set of deliverables:

- Is the set of deliverables complete?

- Does each deliverable work?

- Does each deliverable work exactly as you intended and with all the features you expected to be in it?

- Can each deliverable meet the performance needs of the customer? (For example, where appropriate to the deliverable, does it work as quickly as expected, can a large enough number of people use it at any one time, etc.)

- Have the deliverables been made/built/created to the level of quality that was required?

- Are there any specific acceptance criteria or processes that the customer has defined – and have the deliverables met these criteria?

Considering the office relocation project used in Chapters 3 and 4, the test might be to check that:

- There actually are 100 desks, chairs and sufficient supporting infrastructure installed.

- Each combination of desk, chair and infrastructure is arranged so that every member of staff can use them comfortably and effectively.

- Each desk has adequate lighting and power points.

- The wireless can be easily and quickly linked to – both for the internal secure network, and for the public guest network.

- The wireless network continues to work effectively when over 100 devices are connected simultaneously to it.

There is some more detailed information on testing in 'Taking it further' at the end of this step.

Key drivers for success **9** **Remain closely involved in the work**

Project management is a hands-on task. To be able to manage a project well you have to have an up-to-date view of the status. You need to know accurately how the project is progressing, what problems have occurred today and whether they can easily be resolved or not. You should keep a feeling for how the team are doing: are they enjoying the work and finding it easy, or are they struggling and in need of motivation?

The only way you can achieve this is to remain closely involved in the work. Some project managers take a very hands-off approach and spend their time in the office pouring over the Project Plan or thinking about what needs to happen next. Yes, you need to make sure you have a good plan and, yes, you need time to think, but in the end successful project management is about action. Any action is most effective when it is taken at the appropriate time and usually this is as early as possible. To be able to do this on a project you need to be deeply involved in the project and be aware of what is going on.

Step 5.2 Implement deliverables

Now that your deliverables work properly, you must implement them. For some deliverables, implementing is just about giving them to a customer, but for others they need to be made to work with existing items. (For example, loading new software on to a customer's IT systems – the software needs to work with or not interfere with any software already in use.) Also, how the deliverable works or can be used needs to be shown to the customer.

There are many ways to implement deliverables, and it does depend on the type of deliverable. Typically the questions you need to ask to implement any deliverable are:

- Are your customers ready for the deliverables? For example, if you are going to install a new set of furniture in an office, is the office available or is it full of people busily doing their normal work who cannot be currently disturbed?

- Are the deliverables something completely new or do they replace something the customer already has? If the latter, how are you going to help them make the transition from what they currently have to what you have developed? Consider the situation in which the deliverable from the project is a new set of pricing and discounting rules for a company's salesforce that describes a new way to sell a new product you have developed. How are you going to ensure that the salesforce read, understand and follow these rules instead of the existing ones?

- Do the deliverables need to be integrated or made to work with anything else? Who is responsible for doing this and how will it be done? Imagine the situation that you are delivering a new machine into a factory. If this machine works alone, then you simply need to find space and a power supply for it. But what if the machine has to work with another existing machine: who is going to fit the two machines together and check that they work properly together?

- Do the deliverables need any specific actions to implement? What are these and who will do them? Some deliverables can only be implemented in a special way. If your deliverable is some new computer software, how is it to be installed onto everyone's computers? Who will do this?

- Does your customer need to be trained? If so, how is this training going to be provided? Consider a project in which you are delivering a new set of work instructions for staff in a call centre.

The project has developed the instructions, but now the staff, who must follow the instructions, need to have the instructions explained to them, and someone must make sure the staff understand the instructions fully.

There is some more information on implementation in the 'Taking it further' at the end of this step.

Step 5.3 Provide support to your customers

The deliverables are now being used by the customers. However, the customers still may not understand every feature of them. Also customers can come across problems that only appear when the deliverables are in daily use. This means you may need to provide support to your customers for a short period after completing the project. Ask yourself:

● Are the customers likely to have any problems with your deliverables once you have handed them over?

● How will you resolve these issues?

● How will you know when this period of support is complete?

Supporting your customer after you finish a project is good practice, but you can risk a situation in which your project never ends. To avoid the trap of never being able to finish a project, agree up front with your customer how long you will provide support for. This period of time should be built into the Project Plan.

In the example of the office move in Chapters 3 and 4, you may decide you need to provide some newly recruited staff support as they get used to their roles in the new office, and you may want to engage your new customers. In providing support you may want to ensure:

● Each member of staff knows which is their desk, and their way around the office facilities including fire escapes, toilets, printers and the coffee area.

● There is help for anyone who needs to locate the packing cases that contain their files, or who wants to raise or lower their chairs, or link to the wireless network.

Step 5.4 Release resources

As people complete the tasks on the Project Plan you required them to do, you can release them from the project team. However, do not do this prematurely. People should only be released from the team when:

1. You are sure that they have completed all the tasks required. This is not simply that they have worked until a certain date specified in the plan has passed. It is not only a date that needs to have passed, but that all the work they were meant to do has been completed.

2. You have confidence you will not need them to help you test and implement the deliverables, or provide any further support to the customer.

The other resource you may have left is money. Hopefully you have not spent more than your original budget (including contingency). Assuming there is some money left, you need to give this back to your customer, or at least alert the company accountant that all that is going to be spent has been spent.

Key drivers for success	10	Consider what happens *after* the project

Projects are temporary endeavours to achieve an outcome. After the project is complete, if you are a project manager, you will probably move on to another project. What matters after the project is complete is how well the outcome you have achieved and the deliverables you have created continue to be useful to the project customer.

What happens after the project is actually more important than what happens during the project. A really well-run project comes to an end cleanly and precisely, and for a long time afterwards the deliverables work as they were intended.

There is a risk that project managers and project teams can become so focused on finishing the project that they lose sight of what happens after the project. If your project was to decorate the house, then what matters most is not

▶

finishing the decorating, but how well that decoration stands up to being lived in for the years afterwards. If your project was to launch a new product, then what matters most is how well that product sells once the project is complete.

As the project manager you cannot decide what happens after the project, but you can influence the future by doing tasks in the project that mean the future is more likely to be a good one. For example, you can ensure you create deliverables of sufficient quality that they really achieve what they are designed for. You can prepare the customer, as part of the project, to use those deliverables in the best way possible.

Step 5.5 Review for next time

Is this the only project you will ever run? Is this the only project that will ever be run in your business? Normally the answer to both of these questions is no. If that is so, it is worth reviewing the project very soon after it is complete to make sure you have learnt any valuable lessons. Don't leave a long period before doing this review as you need the memory of the project to be fresh in your mind.

The main questions to answer in performing a review are:

- *What will you continue to do?* What went well and what will you do again on your next project?

- *What will you stop doing?* What went badly and what will you do differently on your next project?

- *What will you start doing?* What didn't you do on this project that in hindsight would have been good to do?

- *Is there anything else* you have learnt that is worth remembering for next time?

This review should involve the project team – and if you can, the project customer as well.

Key drivers for success	**11**	All experiences are an opportunity to learn

It takes time and experience to become a really good project manager. Some people find it easier to learn the tools, techniques and habits of the project manager. Anyone can learn to be a project manager, but only if you really make the effort to learn. Every experience on a project – good, bad or indifferent – is an opportunity to learn and develop your skills further. Think about how and why you achieved the outcome you did, and use those lessons on future projects. That way you will become a better project manager.

Step 5.6 Celebrate!

Finishing a project successfully should be something you are proud of. If you have followed the steps in this book, you will now understand that the underlying principles of project management are really not that complex and in some ways are just common sense applied in a structured way. Yet managing projects well is something many people struggle with and often fail at. If you have completed your project successfully, you and the project team deserve a celebration.

Key tips

- Consider whether the deliverables from your project need to be tested and implemented, and if they do how you are going to do this.

- Be prepared, if necessary, to provide some support to your customer for a short period after the deliverables have been implemented.

- Control the release of people from the project.

- Don't forget to celebrate your success!

- Build your Project Plan and Project Budget to include the necessary tasks in this chapter.

- If you are running late, or short of budget, avoid the temptation to skip these tasks.

TO DO NOW

- Review your Project Plan. Ask yourself, is there anything else you need to do to make sure your customer will really benefit from the results of the project?

- Make sure you have built all these tasks into the Project Plan and Project Budget, and that you have people in the project team allocated to these tasks.

Conclusion

Now you have completed the core parts of *Project Management Step-by-Step*. If you follow the steps in this book you can manage a project.

You started in Chapter 1 by building up your vocabulary and under-standing of simple project management concepts. Then in Chapter 2 you learnt how to clearly define the objective of a project in a Project Definition. By following the activities in Chapter 3 you learnt how to build a Project Plan, and by following Chapter 4 you saw how to man-age a project. Chapter 5 showed you how to ensure your project finishes successfully. Supporting these chapters were the 'Key drivers for suc-cess', which highlight the best styles of working to achieve your project goals.

There is more than this book covers to being a really great project man-ager, who can deliver the largest and most complex of projects. However in most situations, what is in this book, if applied well, will greatly enhance your chances of success. Reference the material here as often as you need to.

The more you practise, the better your skills as a project manager will become. Project management is a practical rather than a theoretical sub-ject. Read the book, then try out the advice in reality. Review what hap-pened after every project and learn from your successes and your mistakes. When you have the opportunity, observe others and learn from them too.

For now though you have completed the core steps in this step-by-step guide, and you should be proud that you know how to manage projects. It's an ability most people lack. Good luck and enjoy it!

What if you liked the process so much that you want to learn more about project management? At the end of each chapter, including this one, is some additional optional reading material titled 'Taking it further' aimed at those who want to use this book as a starting point for a move into a project management career. There is also an extensive glossary to reference.

Taking it further: Testing, integration, implementation and quality management

In this final step I touched on the need to test and implement the deliverables from your project. There is an additional stage to consider as well, and that is integration. For major projects the topics of testing, integration and implementation need specialist resources and significant time to complete. Poor testing, integration and implementation are often the basis of project failure. Associated with them is *quality management*. These are four large topics, which cannot be covered in the context of this book, and this section simply gives a brief introductory overview of them.

Testing is a large subject and a specialist discipline in its own right. There are, for example, people and teams whose sole role is to perform testing on complex projects such as major software developments. There are many types of testing for different types of deliverables. Generically the types of testing tend to fall into the following five categories:

1. *Testing for completeness.* Do you have all the deliverables you expect to have?

2. *Functionality testing.* Does each deliverable do what it is meant to do?

3. *Quality testing.* Is each deliverable of the quality level required? Quality can be measured in many ways, but would include issues such as reliability.

4. *Usability testing.* Is each deliverable in a form that can be used easily by the customer, and that they are happy with?

5. *Operational testing.* When a deliverable is used in the real world, does it work as expected and can it be operated without disrupting everything else it interacts with?

The process of formal testing has to be very rigorous and highly structured. To pass, a deliverable is checked against a very specific and predefined set of tests. These tests are written in a document called a *test specification*. Ideally this test specification was written at a similar time to the requirements and is a mirror document to it. For every requirement there should be a corresponding test step.

This is reasonably straightforward if the deliverables from your project are distinct and complete deliverables in their own right. However, often there are multiple deliverables which have to work together. Bringing many deliverables together and making them work seamlessly is called *integration* or *systems integration*. For example, if your project is to build a new gear box for a kit car you have built, then at some point you must integrate the gear box with the rest of the car's engine. Similarly, if you have developed a piece of software it often has to work with other pieces of software, including the operating system. Without trying to explain the mechanics of integration, which are complex and depend on the specific type of deliverables, there are three important things for the project manager to understand:

1. Where integration must happen, it is a distinct task that takes time and resources. It needs to be built into the Project Plan and shown as a separate series of activities.

2. Integration is only possible if the various component deliverables have been designed to be integrated. The gear box for your kit car cannot be designed any way you like, it has to be designed to work with the rest of your car's engine. This may sound very obvious, but it is common for complex deliverables to fail when it comes to integration.

3. Integration will not happen by itself, someone with the necessary skills has to do it. Simply having people on the project team responsible for building all the individual component deliverables is not enough, you have to have someone responsible for overseeing the integration itself.

Once a set of deliverables is integrated and shown to be working, it is ready to be implemented. In a normal business environment, the deliverables from any one project must be made to work with the people who work there. For example, a new computer system has to be explained to the people who must use it. Deliverables such as new computer systems, new processes for working, new organisational structures are changes to the way people work. For such changes to be successful, they need to be willingly adopted by the people involved. If you look at many business disputes, and major project failures in the press, they are often because of failed or poorly implemented changes.

The art of getting people to adopt new deliverables and ways of working is normally called *change management*. At the very simplest, this means the bringing of deliverables into a working environment. It also encompasses training people to use them. One of the most challenging pieces of change management is preparing people for the change that new deliverables bring about, and overcoming any objections so that they work entirely successfully. Change management is not something that happens at the end of a project, it needs to happen throughout the life of a project. When the project completes, all the preparation has been done and thus the change can be implemented smoothly.

When you consider testing, integration and implementation all together, you can get a series of test stages that need to be built into the plan for your project, such as:

1. *Unit test.* When the individual deliverables from the project are tested.

2. *Integration test.* When the deliverables are tested together as a complete working system.

3. *User acceptance test.* When the end users of the system test to see whether it works as they expected.

4. *Operations test.* When the integrated deliverables are tested within the live operational environment to ensure they work in the real world.

To put these activities into perspective, for a major programme of work the stages of testing, integration and implementation may take 30 per cent or more of the total length of the project.

An important concept to understand is project *Quality Management*, usually divided into *QA* (*Quality Assurance*) and *QC* (*Quality Control*). Essentially, Quality Assurance is concerned with ensuring you are using the right processes in the project – that is, processes that have been shown to deliver a reliable result and reduce the risk of problems or defects with project deliverables. QA may be ensured by audits of a project to check how it is being run. Quality Control is concerned with checking deliverables to ensure they are fit for purpose once they have been produced. It is focused on removing defects from deliverables. Testing is a good example of QC.

FURTHER READING

- **Implementation:** Newton, R., *The Theory and Practice of Project Management*, Palgrave Macmillan, 2010

- **Project Quality Management:** Rose, K., *Project Quality Management: Why, What, How*, 2nd Edition, J Ross Publishing, 2014

- **Change management:** Newton, R., *Managing Change Step-by-Step*, Pearson Education, 2007

Glossary

This glossary provides a summary of the project management terminology used in this book. It also describes jargon commonly used in project management circles that has not been referred to in this book. You may come across this jargon when talking to others involved in projects. If you want to work in the project domain or with project managers this is useful to know.

All the definitions are my own and are specific to the context of project management. The descriptions reflect everyday usage of the term, rather than formally agreed definitions, which do not always reflect common usage.

Agile

Agile is a way of delivering projects that differs from traditional project management – using very short rapid iterative development techniques and applying different tools and techniques. It originated following the *Agile Manifesto*, written in 2001. It initially became important as a technique used in software development (and especially web developments). But increasingly it is spreading out as the approach for a wide variety of projects.

It is worth differentiating between **A**gile and **a**gile. Agile (noun, capital A) is the name of the delivery methodology referred to here. In comparison agile (adjective, lower case a) is a generally used word in business referring to the ease with which an organisation can implement change – as in 'an agile organisation'.

Association of Project Managers (APM)

The APM is a UK-based professional body for project managers, promoting good practice in project management. It provides various levels of membership and certification for a variety of project management disciplines.

Assumption

An assumption is a conjecture about the future made on a project. Assumptions are made when a project team needs some information to progress, and does not currently have the ability to determine the information. Assumptions enable projects to progress without getting held up every time there is an unknown, but assumptions increase risk as there is always a chance the assumptions are wrong. Key assumptions should be reflected in the risk management process.

Backlog

A backlog is a term used in Agile for the prioritised list of stories related to the overall goal of an Agile team (sufficient and necessary to meet the goal). The backlog is used to agree the specific stories that will be delivered in the next iteration or sprint.

Benefit

The value a project sets out to achieve. Generally, benefits are achieved by the use of the deliverables from a project. For example, if the deliverable is a new software system, the benefits are the value gained from using this software.

Benefits realisation

The process of ensuring a project meets the objective (the 'why') it was originally designed to meet. Benefits realisation tracks and optimises the achievement of benefits.

Business analysis/business analyst

Business analysis is the formal discipline of exploring business problems and needs, identifying solutions and capturing those solutions in the form of requirements. A business analyst is someone with expertise in business analysis.

Business rationale/business objective

The objective of a business project (the 'why') – usually used to justify any expenditure or the allocation of resources from a project. This is usually defined in monetary terms as a measure of the benefit the project customer will gain by investing in the project.

Change

A change is an alteration to one of the five dimensions (*see* Project dimensions definition) of a project. In a project a change should be a deliberate choice and not simply an accidental result of some other action. (Change has an alternative meaning referring to the impact of a project – *see* Change management). Unless project managers control change they cannot reliably achieve the project plan.

Change control

Change control is the project management process for managing alterations to project requirements, scope or other dimension.

Change management

Change management is the process for identifying, assessing, implementing and managing the impact of the change a project brings about. For example, if a project implements new processes in a business, change management is concerned with ensuring the new processes are used properly and result in the desired benefits. Change management involves many activities to prepare people for change, such as training and communications. It should not be confused with change control.

Communications plan

A communications plan is an identifiable subset of a project plan concerned with the communication tasks in a project. Many projects require communication to stakeholders to ensure engagement in the project and acceptance of its deliverables.

Contingency

A buffer, in the form of time and money, held by the project manager. Contingency is in addition to the time and money required to complete the project, as shown by the project plan. Contingency is used to manage the risk from unpredicted events occurring on a project, and the amount of contingency should be a function of how much risk there is associated with the project.

Crashing

Crashing refers to a variety of project schedule compression techniques. This is performed to decrease total project duration.

Critical chain

Critical chain is a way of managing projects that derives from the writing of Eliyahu Goldratt, intended to overcome some of the problems arising from other project management techniques.

Critical path

The sequence of tasks on a plan that determines the length of time a project will take. If any task on the critical path is extended – the project will extend. Alternatively, to shorten the project you must shorten the critical path. Critical path analysis identifies the critical path with the aim of reducing it.

Daily stand-up

Daily stand-ups are brief project team meetings, usually held at the start of the day. The name derives from the idea that the meeting should be held standing up to encourage brevity. At the stand-up project team members quickly outline what they are working on and any issues they have. If issues or work needs to be discussed in any detail, this is done outside of the daily stand-up. Daily stand-ups are usually associated with Agile, but which can be used on any project.

Decomposition

The process of breaking a (complex) activity into smaller component tasks to allow it to be better understood. It may also be used to break down complex deliverables into smaller, more easily understandable deliverables.

Delivery

The completion of a project, or the activity of working to complete a project, within the defined conditions – usually the creation of the expected deliverables from a project within the time and cost expected.

Deliverables

What a project develops or produces, also sometimes called the outputs from a project.

Dependency

A dependency is a relationship between tasks in a project plan. There are many forms of dependency. The most common is a start-to-finish dependency, where one task cannot start until another finishes. For example, the testing tasks in a project plan cannot start until the creation of deliverables has been completed – as it is those deliverables being tested.

Dimensions

See Project dimensions.

Duration

The elapsed time from the start to finish for a task. Duration includes both the time a task is being actively worked on (*see* Effort), plus any delays or time waiting between the start and finish of the task.

Earned value

A project management technique used to track project progress by measuring the value delivered at points in the project's lifecycle.

Effort

The amount of time one individual would need to actively work on a task to complete it.

Estimate

The predicted resources a task, group of tasks or whole project plan will take. This may be in terms of time, people or money. For instance, 'the project is estimated to take two years and cost £5 million'.

External dependency

A dependency a project has on some activities outside the scope of the project. Such activities need to be tracked by the project manager, but are not managed or delivered by the project.

Gantt chart

A Gantt chart is the name for a way of presenting project plans. It was devised by Henry Gantt, an early pioneer in project management. Gantt charts are the typical way of presenting plans in traditional project management approaches – with the tasks written in a column on the left-hand side of the page and bars representing the duration of those tasks across the page.

Gate

A gate is a decision point in a project, usually between defined project stages at which project sponsors review the situation and decide whether to allow the project to proceed to the next stage (sometimes called go/no-go decisions). At a gate the decision may be to proceed, or to ask for further work to be done to meet defined conditions before progressing. Occasionally, at a gate the decision may be made to terminate the project.

Governance

Project governance is the framework in which project decisions are made. Such decisions include approving gate decisions, budget decisions, project approach and aligning the project with an organisation's strategy. Governance consists of processes, guidelines and responsibilities – such as the responsibilities of the project's steering committee.

Impediment

An impediment is the name for an issue in the Agile methodology. It refers to anything that slows down or gets in the way of the team progressing their work.

Implementation

The activity of using the deliverables from a project and making them work within a live/operational environment. Implementation covers a wide range of activities but includes tasks such as user familiarity/training users, and introducing deliverables into operational environments such as an office or factory.

Iron triangle

A commonly used rule of thumb used to discuss project dimensions. The triangle is made up of cost, time and quality. The iron triangle is used to indicate that if you can affect any one of these you will have an effect on the others. For example, you cannot decrease the time a project is to be completed in without either changing the cost or the quality of the project. It was originally described by Dr Martin Barnes. (See Project dimensions.)

Issue

An issue is a problem that occurs during a project that has a negative impact on the progress of the project.

Issue management

Issue management is a project management process for the identification and resolution of issues.

Iterative

A technique in which deliverables are created, handed over to customers and improved incrementally. (Contrast with waterfall.) Iterative projects typically have multiple phases until deliverables reach their final desired end state. Agile is a form of iterative development.

Lessons learnt

A project management term for the lessons that have been learnt during a project. These are usually both concerned with improvements that can be made on future projects, as well as things that have gone well and should be repeated on future projects. Although some lessons will be learnt informally as a project progresses, there is usually a review at the end of a project in which the lessons learnt are formally identified and documented for future projects.

Levelling

Levelling or resource levelling, is a technique used to match the start and end dates of a project to the resources available – aiming to balance resource supply with resource demand. Typically, project managers start out producing an ideal plan which takes no account of resource constraints. But a realistic plan must reflect what resources are actually available. It's also helpful to try and keep the resources involved in a project consistently busy across the project lifecycle. This is where levelling is used.

Lifecycle

A generic, high-level description of the stages a project goes through.

Managing Successful Programs (MSP)

The sister methodology and certification programme to Prince 2. MSP is a methodology for programme management.

Milestone

The identification of the completion of a visible and verifiable stage of a project. Milestones are used to track and communicate on progress at a high level.

MoSCoW

A simple guide to help prioritising requirements relative to available resources in a project. MoSCoW represents **M**ust do, **S**hould do, **C**ould do, and **W**ould do.

Opportunity

An opportunity is a positive risk – that is the chance that things might go better in a project than planned or expected.

PERT

Program **E**valuation **R**eview **T**echnique is a way to analyse and present the tasks involved in completing a project.

Plan

The description of the tasks in a project mapped against the time they will take, and usually against the people or teams responsible for them. There are different formats and types of project plans. Plans are used to analyse, schedule, communicate and manage projects.

Portfolio

In project management a portfolio is the name for the collection of projects and programmes being run within the organisation. (Some organisations have multiple portfolios separating projects in different business domains.)

Portfolio management

Portfolio management is concerned with the optimisation of an organisation's portfolio of projects. The goal of portfolio management is to ensure the optimal set of projects is run within an organisation relative to the available resources. Typical tasks in portfolio management are prioritising projects, approving projects to start and resource balancing across projects.

Product owner

The product owner is a key role in Agile. The product owner acts as the main stakeholder for a project and the single point of interface for project customers. The product owner performs a variety of tasks and critically prioritises the backlog.

Prince 2

A well-known project management methodology. Prince 2 stands for **PR**ojects **IN** **C**ontrolled **E**nvironments, version **2**. It is also a certification programme for project managers, with various levels of accreditation. It was originally produced for the UK government.

Programme

A programme is an especially large or complex project, usually in the form of a set of interdependent projects that together achieve some common objective. (Spelt 'program' in the United States). Although there are formal definitions, in practice the term is used inconsistently. Sometimes it refers to what is simply a large project and on other occasions to groups of interrelated projects.

Programme manager

Someone performing the task of programme management. The programme manager on a programme is analogous to the project manager on a project, although the scope of the work is broader.

Programme management

Programme management is an advanced form of project management used to manage programmes, and is exercised by a programme manager.

Progress report

A regularly produced report explaining the status of the project. There are many formats and a variety of purposes. Typically a progress report tells stakeholders how well a project is doing and highlights issues and risks they should be aware of. Also known as status reports.

Project

An activity, with a known and clearly defined goal, that can be achieved. When the defined goal is achieved, the project is complete and ends. Usually a project has to be completed within a fixed amount of time and for a fixed amount of money.

Project customer

The person (or set of people) for whom a project is done. Typically, a customer defines the project requirements, pays for the project and receives the deliverables from a project once it is complete. By using the deliverables the customer hopes to achieve some (business) benefit.

Project dimensions

A project has five dimensions – the **scope** of the project, the **quality** of the deliverables produced and the work done to produce them, the length of **time** it will take, the amount it will **cost** to complete, and the level of **risk** taken in completing the project. These five dimensions are not separate, but are a set of interdependent variables that can be explicitly and deliberately traded off against each other to tailor a project to a customer's needs.

Some commentators suggest projects have alternative dimensions. The iron triangle (see definition above) suggests only three. Other models suggest more.

Project manager

The person with overall responsibility for ensuring a project is delivered.

Project management

A set of experience-based rules, lifecycles, processes, tools and techniques used by a project manager to deliver a project.

Project Management Institute (PMI)

A professional membership association for the project, programme and portfolio management profession. It operates worldwide and originated in the United States.

Project management office (PMO)

The term PMO is applied in a variety of ways to refer to a group who either supports an individual project or set of projects in an organisation. In project management theory the role is meant to define and maintain standards for project management, but roles in practice vary considerably. A PMO may be involved in one or more of the following: project resourcing, portfolio management, collecting and consolidating status reports, defining project management process, consolidating plans across projects or QA'ing projects (*see* Quality Assurance and Quality Control definition).

Project management professional (PMP)

A well-recognised level of project management accreditation devised and promoted by the PMI.

Project sponsor

The sponsor is the person with overall accountability for the delivery of a project. The sponsor is usually a part-time role, directing and supporting the project manager. Sponsors are typically senior and may chair the project's steering committee. Sponsors are usually involved in approving budgets, decision-making and helping to manage senior stakeholders.

Project team

The combined set of people who work on a project, under the management of the project manager.

Quality Assurance and Quality Control (QA and QC)

QA and QC are the two parts of project quality management. Quality Assurance is concerned with ensuring you are using the right processes in the project – that is, processes that have been shown to deliver a reliable result and reduce the risk of problems or defects with project deliverables. Quality Control is concerned with checking deliverables to ensure they are fit for purpose once they have been produced. It is focused on removing defects from deliverables.

RACI

A specific way of identifying who needs to do what on a project. The roles on the project are mapped against the tasks required and then it is identified whether a role is **R**esponsible, **A**ccountable, **C**onsulted or Informed about specific tasks.

RAID log

A RAID log is one way of keeping key data concerning a project. RAID stands for **R**isk, **A**ssumption, **I**ssue and **D**ecision. RAID logs are often kept as spreadsheets with one worksheet for each of the four types of data.

Requirement

What stakeholders want and need from a project. Requirements are formally identified, collected, documented and prioritised through the process of business analysis. A project sets out to fulfil some requirements. It is important to note that just because a requirement exists does not mean the project will fulfil it. This depends on the project's scope and the priority and relevance associated with a particular requirement, as well as the cost of fulfilling it.

Resources

Resource is the project management term for the supplies or inputs a project uses to enable it to produce the outputs or deliverables. The most common resources are money or budget and people or the project team.

Retrospective

A technique, most commonly associated with Agile, for regularly reviewing a project and improving ways of working in the team. In Agile there is a retrospective at the end of each sprint.

Risk

A risk is a prediction that an issue that has not yet occurred will occur – measured in terms of the likelihood (or probability) it will occur and impact if it does.

Risk management

Risk management is the project management process for predicting and managing risks in advance of them becoming issues, and for identifying and leveraging opportunities.

Scope

A formal description and definition of what is (and what is not) within the work of a project – also referred to in this book as the 'what'.

Scope creep

The tendency for the scope of a project to incrementally increase. Scope creep is something project managers need to be alert to. Typically, scope only increases with minor changes. Each change in itself is usually manageable within the project constraints, but the cumulative effect of many changes results in an unachievable project.

Scrum

A specific and widely applied variant of Agile, most commonly used in software development, but increasingly used more widely.

Specification

A specification is a detailed description of some aspect of a project, usually in a documented form. Typical usage is for the description of requirements or the design of deliverables – hence requirements specification or design specification.

Stakeholder

Stakeholder is a broader term than customer, and means anyone with an interest in a project. The project customer is one type of stakeholder.

Stakeholder management

The project management discipline for assessing stakeholder management needs and views. This is typically only relevant for larger projects which can have an effect on many people, or which many people have an interest in and may have an impact on the progress of the project.

Status report

See Progress report.

Steering committee

A group of senior project stakeholders who meet on a periodic basis to execute project governance. Typically, a steering committee makes decisions, approves budgets and tracks project status on behalf of the organisation undertaking the project.

Story

A story or user story is the name for a requirement in Agile. An Agile sprint will fulfil certain prioritised stories. Stories have a specific way of being defined, which is different from traditional project requirements.

Task

An individual activity within a project plan.

Testing

The structured and controlled process of assessing whether the deliverables meet the requirements they were originally specified to meet. (*See* Quality Control.)

VUCA

Volatile, Uncertain, Complex and Ambiguous. This phrase is often used in project management circles to describe the risky environment many projects operate in, and which disciplines such as risk management set out to handle.

Waterfall

The traditional approach to projects, where all the tasks are set out sequentially leading to a single end point, and typically a single hand-over of deliverables to project customers. (Contrast with iterative.)

Work Breakdown Structure (WBS)

A formal description of all the activities required to complete a project, shown as hierarchy of tasks in the project. The WBS is the result of the decomposition of the project into its component tasks.

Work package

A contained sub-component of a project. This is typically only relevant on larger projects which have individual teams focused on different aspects of the project. These different aspects are often called work packages. They are not self-contained projects but usually have significant interdependency between work packages.

Workstream

The set of activities within a project plan related to a specific work package.

Glossary © Richard Newton

Index